THE GREAT COOKS' GUIDE TO
Cakes

GREAT COOKS' LIBRARY
Appetizers
Breads
Cakes
Chickens, Ducks & Other Poultry
Children's Cookery
Clay Cookery
Cookies
Crêpes & Soufflés
Fish Cookery
Flambéing Desserts
Ice Cream & Other Frozen Desserts
Omelets from Around the World
Pasta & Noodle Dishes
Pies & Tarts
Rice Cookery
Salads
Soups
Vegetable Cookery
Wine Drinks
Woks, Steamers & Fire Pots

America's leading food authorities share their home-tested recipes and expertise on cooking equipment and techniques

THE GREAT COOKS' GUIDE TO
Cakes

A BEARD GLASER WOLF BOOK

RANDOM HOUSE, NEW YORK

Front Cover (left to right, top to bottom): Kuglof, page 10.

Back Cover (left to right, top to bottom): Strawberry Mary Ann, page 22; Madeleines, page 13; *(cake stand courtesy Paulette's Place; rubber spatula courtesy Charles F. Lamalle);* Deluxe Chocolate Layer Cake, page 42.

Interior Photographs: Page 6 (top), *angel food pan courtesy H. Roth & Son;* page 6 (bottom), *spatula courtesy Bloomingdale's, turntable courtesy The Professional Kitchen, decorating set courtesy H. Roth & Son.*

Book Design by Milton Glaser, Inc.

Cover Photograph by Richard Jeffery

Food Styling by Lucy Wing
Props selected by Yvonne McHarg and Beard Glaser Wolf Ltd.

Copyright © 1977 by Jay Rosengarten
All rights reserved under International and Pan-American Copyright Conventions. Published in the United States by Beard Glaser Wolf Ltd.

Library of Congress Cataloguing in Publication Data

Main entry under title:

The Great cooks guide to cakes.
(The Great cooks' library)
1. Cake. I. Series.

TX771.G73   641.8'653   77-18389
ISBN 0-394-73605-2

Manufactured in the United States of America
2 4 6 8 9 7 5 3
First Edition

We have gathered together some of the great cooks in this country to share their recipes—and their expertise—with you. As you read the recipes, you will find that in certain cases techniques will vary. This is as it should be: Cooking is a highly individual art, and our experts have arrived at their own personal methods through years of experience in the kitchen.

THE EDITORS

SENIOR EDITORS
Wendy Afton Rieder
Kate Slate

ASSOCIATE EDITORS
Lois Bloom
Susan Lipke

EDITORIAL ASSISTANT
Christopher Carter

WRITER/RESEARCHER
Diana Childress

PRODUCTION MANAGER
Emily Aronson

EDITORIAL STAFF
Mardee Haidin
Michael Sears
Patricia Thomas

CONTRIBUTORS

Bianca Brown, now a freelance food writer, has worked as associate food editor at *Good Housekeeping*, writing the feature, "Foods with a Foreign Flavor," and as associate editor at *Gourmet* magazine.

Paula J. Buchholz is the regional co-ordinator for the National Culinary Apprenticeship Program. She has been a food writer for the *Detroit Free Press* and for the *San Francisco Examiner*.

Ruth Ellen Church, a syndicated wine columnist for the *Chicago Tribune*, had been food editor for that newspaper for more than thirty years when she recently retired. The author of seven cookbooks, her most recent books are *Entertaining with Wine* and *Wines and Cheeses of the Midwest*.

Elizabeth Schneider Colchie is a noted food consultant who has done extensive recipe development and testing as well as research into the history of foods and cookery. She was on the editorial staff of *The Cooks' Catalogue* and *The International Cooks' Catalogue* and has written numerous articles for such magazines as *Gourmet, House & Garden* and *Family Circle*.

Isabel S. Cornell, a home economist, was Associate Editor for the revised edition of *Woman's Day Encyclopedia of Cookery* and Special Projects Editor for the revised edition of *Woman's Day Collector's Cook Book*. While on the *Woman's Day* staff, she selected, tested and judged for their recipe contests.

Carol Cutler, who has been a food columnist for the *Washington Post*, is a graduate of the Cordon Bleu and L'Ecole des Trois Gourmands in Paris. She is the author of *Haute Cuisine for Your Heart's Delight*, and *The Six-Minute Soufflé and Other Culinary Delights*. She has also written for *House & Garden, American Home* and *Harper's Bazaar.*

Rona Deme, a native of England, ran a pork store with her husband for 25 years and in 1972 opened up The Country Host, a gourmet food shop in New York City.

Florence Fabricant is a free-lance writer, reporting on restaurants and food for *The New York Times, New York* magazine and other publications. She was on the staff of *The Cooks' Catalogue* and editor of the paperback edition. She also contributed to *The International Cooks' Catalogue* and *Where to Eat in America.*

Emanuel and Madeline Greenberg co-authored *Whiskey in the Kitchen* and are consultants to the food and beverage industry. Emanuel, a home economist, is a regular contributor to the food columns of *Playboy* magazine. Both contribute to *House Beautiful, Harper's Bazaar* and *Travel & Leisure.*

George and Arthur Herbst own a New York City bakery—started by their parents—called Mrs. Herbst's Homemade Pastries and Strudels.

Mireille Johnston, the author of *The Cuisine of the Sun,* a cookbook of Provençal specialties, is currently completing a book on the cooking of Burgundy, *The Cuisine of the Rose.*

Matt Kramer writes a food column for the *Willamette Week* in Portland, Oregon.

Alma Lach holds a Diplôme de Cordon Bleu from Paris and has served as food editor for the *Chicago Sun-Times*. She is author of *How's and Why's of French Cooking* and *Cooking à la Cordon Bleu* as well as many other cookbooks and articles on food. She directs the Alma Lach Cooking School in Chicago and is currently the television chef on the P.B.S. program "Over Easy."

Linda Lewis is co-founder of Miss Grimble's bakery in New York City and a consultant on new products, recipe development, and menu planning to food companies and restaurants.

Susan Lipke is an Associate Editor of the Great Cooks' Library series as well as *The International Cooks' Catalogue* and *The Cooks' Catalogue*, and writes and tests recipes.

Nan Mabon, a freelance food writer and cooking teacher in New York City, is also the cook for a private executive dining room on Wall Street.

She studied at the Cordon Bleu in London.

Maurice Moore-Betty, owner-operator of The Civilized Art Cooking School, food consultant and restaurateur, is author of *Cooking for Occasions, The Maurice Moore-Betty Cooking School Book of Fine Cooking* and *The Civilized Art of Salad Making.*

Jane Moulton, a food writer for the *Plain Dealer* in Cleveland, took her degree in foods and nutrition. As well as reporting on culinary matters and reviewing food-related books for the *Plain Dealer*, she has worked in recipe development, public relations and catering.

Paul Rubinstein is the author of *Feasts for Two, The Night Before Cookbook* and *Feasts for Twelve (or More).* He is a stockbroker and the son of pianist Artur Rubinstein.

Maria Luisa Scott and Jack Denton Scott co-authored the popular *Complete Book of Pasta* and have also written many other books on food, including *Informal Dinners for Easy Entertaining, Mastering Microwave Cooking, The Best of the Pacific Cookbook,* and *Cook Like a Peasant, Eat Like a King.* With the renowned chef Antoine Gilly, they wrote *Feast of France.*

Raymond Sokolov, author of *The Saucier's Apprentice,* is a freelance writer with a particular interest in food.

Ruth Spear is the author of *The East Hampton Cookbook* and writes occasional pieces on food for *New York* magazine. She is currently at work on a new cookbook.

Marion Lear Swaybill, a field producer-writer in the documentary division of NBC News in New York, long ago took up cooking as a serious avocation and has become an expert cook and baker.

Lucy Wing is a freelance food writer and food photography home economist. She has developed recipes for magazines and food and kitchen equipment companies and has been an editorial contributor to numerous women's magazines, including *Family Circle, Good Housekeeping, McCall's* and *American Home.*

Nicola Zanghi is the owner-chef of Restaurant Zanghi in Glen Cove, New York. He started his apprenticeship under his father at the age of thirteen, and is a graduate of two culinary colleges. He has been an instructor at the Cordon Bleu school in New York City.

Contents

Introduction 1

COFFEE AND TEA CAKES

Kuglof 10
Apple Coffee Cake 11
Panettone 12
Honey and Spice Cakes 12
Madeleines 13
Burnt Sugar Cupcakes 14
Sour Cream Coffee Cake 15
Lemon Glazed Tea Cake 16
Eccles Cake 16
Rum-Raisin Tea Loaf 17
Butterfly Cakes 18

FRUIT CAKES AND CAKES WITH FRUIT

Dundee Cake 19
Dresdner Stollen 20
Banana Upside-Down Cake 21
Strawberry Mary Ann 22
Chocolate Date Cake 23
Blueberry Cheesecake 24
Pear Kuchen 25
Simnel Cake 26
Trifle 27

TORTES, LAYER AND TUBE CAKES

Super Lucious Chocolate Cake 28
Dobos Torte 30
Zuppa Inglese 31
Yogurt Chocolate Cake 32
Sweet Mouthful 32
Walnut Torte 34

Almond Layer Cake ___35
Hazelnut-Cherry Torte ___36
Angel Food with Cream Filling ___37
Peach-Pecan Shortcake-Torte___38
Linzertorte ___39
Black and White Tunnel Cake ___40
Marbled 1, 2, 3, 4 Cake ___40
Mina Thompson's Banana Layer Cake ___41
Deluxe Chocolate Layer Cake___42
Chocolate Walnut Torte ___43
Three-Layer Cake for Two ___44

LOAF, SHEET, ROLLED AND SPECIALTY CAKES

Eggnog Roulade___45
Fresh Ginger Cake___46
Baba au Rhum ___47
Old-Fashioned Carrot Cake ___48
Chocolate Chiffon Cake ___49
Arkansas Special Dessert ___50
Coffee Almond Sponge Cake ___50
Ginger Bread ___51
Chocolate-Moka Hazelnut Cake ___52
Almond Butter Cream Cake___53
Chocolate Swiss Roll___54

Cakes

"I raised to my lips the spoonful of the tea in which I had soaked a morsel of the cake. No sooner had the warm liquid, and the crumbs with it, touched my palate, than a shudder ran through my whole body... an exquisite pleasure had invaded my senses." Thus began Marcel Proust's recollection of the experiences and feelings of his childhood associated with the plump little cake called a *madeleine*. For most of us, such remembrances of things past is likely to occur whenever the aroma of a baking cake wafts from an oven door. The most significant events of our lives—birthdays, weddings, anniversaries and holidays—are times we associate with decorative, delicious cakes. In an increasingly technological age, baking a cake is still a simple, highly personal way to express love, appreciation, congratulations or warm hospitality. Remember that old song, "If I'd known you were comin' I'd a baked a cake"? What guest doesn't feel just a bit special when an attractive cake is presented in his or her honor?

Yet with the 20th-century invention of cake mixes, many of us have failed to more than dabble in the imaginative realm of cake baking. Sad, for baking from scratch takes far less time and effort than one might think, and fresh ingredients can make an enormous difference. Mixes, designed for longevity, may sit for as long as two years on a supermarket shelf. A homemade creation with fresh ingredients will taste far better.

There's really no mystery to cake baking. The most important trick is this: Follow the recipe. Each instruction is there for a reason, and failure to heed what may seem a small step—like greasing or not greasing the pans—will affect the final product. From ingredients to equipment to techniques, the recipe should rule.

The Rise to Success. There is one basic ingredient, however, that many recipes neglect to mention. Knowing what it is and how to handle it will help ensure any cake's success. That ingredient is air. To give cake its lightness, air must be pampered into the batter and kept there. For some cakes, most of the air is introduced before the batter reaches the oven; in others, a leavening agent such as baking powder or baking soda does most of its work in the oven. The air expands in the hot oven, and causes the cake to "rise." As the batter cooks, the egg proteins and gluten (the elastic substance in flour) forms walls to permanently trap the air.

Many of the principles and techniques of cake baking are devoted to the production and preservation of this elusive commodity. For example, knowing how to properly cream, stir, beat, fold and whip air into a batter is important. But knowing when to *stop* beating is even more so: An *over-beaten* batter will have given up its much sought after air.

The ingredients that cause a cake to rise are very often what gives it its own special characteristics. So-called "foam" cakes—sponge and angel food, for example—are leavened by eggs alone. Angel food cakes use whites only and are very light; slightly heavier sponge cakes use the yolks as well. Unlike foam cakes, "butter" cakes have shortening as well as eggs and their heavier batters need help from an agent such as baking powder in order to rise. Then there are yeast-risen cakes—like Italian *panettone*, Middle-European *Kugelhopf* or French *baba*—that walk a thin line between cake and bread.

Ingredients. Since an inspirational rainy afternoon or unexpected guest cannot be planned for exactly, it's a good idea to keep the basic ingredients always at hand. Most of them are staples anyway: Fresh dairy products—eggs, milk and butter—as well as flour, baking powder, flavorings and sugar, which will keep almost indefinitely if stored in tight containers.

Eggs give cake flavor, color and texture. Unless otherwise specified, most recipes use large eggs. For baking purposes, they should be at least three days old. Eggs just out of the refrigerator separate best, but at room temperature (75 F.) they can be beaten to much greater volumes. Do not beat eggs until just before they're needed.

Butter is the most common shortening used in cakes. It should be very fresh and unless the recipe specifies otherwise, softened, not melted, before using. Margarine may be substituted in equal quantities for butter. Vegetable shortening, on the other hand, unlike butter and margarine, is 100 percent fat: If substituting it for butter, use only four-fifths of the amount called for.

Two kinds of flour are used in cake baking. The all-purpose variety, a blend of soft and hard wheats, will do for most recipes. Cake flour, a finely-milled soft wheat flour, produces a delicate, more crumbly texture. Pre-sifted and self-rising flours should be avoided. The former won't produce cakes of as fine a grain as sift-yourself types; the latter won't leaven properly if it's not absolutely fresh. If a recipe specifies cake flour, all-purpose flour can be substituted; but for each cup of cake flour required, use one cup minus two tablespoons of the heavier all-purpose type. In addition, when all-purpose flour is substituted for cake flour, be careful not to overbeat the batter. The higher gluten content of all-purpose flour may toughen the cake.

The types of sugar used in cake baking are granulated, brown, superfine and confectioners'. Granulated is the most common sweetener, and brown sugar is used to add a darker, treacley flavor. Unless otherwise specified, brown sugar should be firmly packed when it's measured. Superfine sugar (sometimes called berry sugar) is especially good for sweetening egg whites or heavy cream because it dissolves more quickly than all the others. Confectioners' sugar (which contains a small amount of cornstarch) is used to dust cakes and make icings. It should never be substituted for other sugars.

Baking powder, an invention of the early 19th century, is a combination of bicarbonate of soda (baking soda) and an acidic substance which reacts chemically with the liquid in a batter to produce carbon dioxide. The escaping gas causes the cake to rise. Double-acting baking powder (the most common type available) ensures that the baking powder will not do all its fizzing in the cold batter, but saves some action for the actual baking. To make sure that baking powder has not gone stale, dissolve some in water; if it doesn't bubble, don't use it.

Although most recipes call for baking powder, recipes with acid ingredients like sour milk or sour cream often call for baking soda; as with baking powder, the soda and acid combine to give off carbon dioxide. Baking soda can be used in place of baking powder in the following way: For every teaspoon of baking powder required, use ¼ teaspoon soda plus ½ cup buttermilk or sour milk (in place of another liquid ingredient).

Yeast consists of tiny living organisms that feed on sugar to produce the carbon dioxide needed to make dough rise. It comes in compressed and dried forms. Dried yeast, sold in moisture-proof packages, keeps several months; compressed cakes of fresh yeast keep only a few weeks and should be stored in the refrigerator.

Some form of liquid will be part of any cake recipe. Acidic liquids —sour milk, yogurt, citrus juices, coffee—break down the gluten in flour and produce a softer cake. A tablespoon of vinegar or lemon juice added to a cup of sweet milk will sour it in five minutes.

Chocolate, unsweetened or semisweet, should be melted in a double boiler or in a low oven and cooled before it is mixed into cake batter. Cocoa (the dark, unsweetened Dutch type is best) can be substituted for solid chocolate: Three tablespoons of cocoa plus a tablespoon of butter equals an ounce of unsweetened chocolate.

Nuts add both flavor and texture to a cake. To make delicate, crumbly tortes, finely ground nuts are used in place of flour. They can be purchased already ground or, better still, ground at home with a nut grinder. Although blenders and food processors will grind nuts, they also batter them about, which extracts oils. A nut grinder, on the other hand, shaves the nuts, producing a flakier, more floury consistency. When adding large pieces or whole nuts to a batter, dredge them first in flour and add them just before the batter is poured into the baking pans: This keeps them from sinking.

Vanilla is the most common cake flavoring. Buy vanilla *extract* (not vanillin, a synthetic flavoring) and be sure to add it only to cooled ingredients, or it will lose much of its flavor. Other extracts (natural, of course), liqueurs and hard spirits are all cake enhancers.

Equipment. Good equipment is as important as fresh ingredients. For measuring, a set of metal measuring cups for dry ingredients, a clear glass or plastic measuring cup for liquid ingredients and a set of metal measuring spoons are essential. Flour should be sifted before measuring. A triple-screened sifter is best. A nut grinder will grind nuts for tortes. In small amounts of about ¼ cup at a time, a blender or food processor can also be used to grind nuts, if watched carefully.

For mixing, an electric mixer will save lots of elbow grease, particularly when making rich, creamed cakes. Some mixers have sophisticated attachments that will perform all the mixing motions, including a large wire beater that functions as a balloon whisk. An extra set of beaters and bowls will also come in handy. A long-handled wooden spoon, a wire whisk or two (thin and balloon size), and a rubber spatula will still be needed, for some creaming, beating and folding tasks are better done by hand. A pastry brush and a flour dredger make speedy preparation of baking pans. Since the wrong temperature can ruin a cake, an oven thermometer is a good investment. And wire racks are essential: Exposing cakes fully to the air as they cool keeps them from getting soggy.

Pans. The best cake pans are made of shiny, heavy-gauge tinned steel. Glass, enameled, or dark-colored pans absorb more heat and can dry out the cake or burn the outside. To compensate for the additional heat when using any of these pans, lower the oven temperature by 25 degrees.

All pans should be clean, smooth and unwarped. A dent or a streak of burned-on grease can cause a cake to burn, overbake or tear. If a pan won't come clean, the bottom should be insulated for baking with several layers of greased paper.

To bake a variety of cakes requires a variety of pans: Round layer pans, an angel food cake pan, a regular tube pan, a muffin pan and a loaf pan. A jelly-roll pan will produce a flat cake that can be rolled up with a filling. The cake can also be divided into three sections to make a layered stack with a filling, or it can be cut into squares and diamonds for petit fours. Delicate cakes like tortes and cheesecake are best baked in a springform pan from which they can easily be removed: By releasing a clamp, the sides of the pan spring free of the cake.

Pans also come in special shapes. A Mary Ann pan has a raised circular platform in the center that makes a depression in the finished cake to hold a wealth of fruit, custard and/or whipped cream. For a traditional German *Kugelhopf* (or Austrian *Gugelhupf* or Hungarian *Kuglof*), there's a mold with gracefully swirled fluting around the sides. *Madeleines* get their characteristic shape from a pan with scallop shell indentations.

Preparation. Take the eggs, butter and milk out of the refrigerator about 20 minutes before starting the recipe. Separate the eggs, if required. Turn on the oven and assemble all the necessary ingredients and equipment. This way everything will be at your fingertips and the egg whites won't flop while you search for a spatula to fold them into the batter.

Prepare the pans as the recipe specifies. For cakes made with shortening, the pans are usually greased with butter and dusted with flour or fine bread crumbs. But for cakes with little or no fat, like angel food and sponge cakes, the pan must be grease-free, otherwise the batter won't rise. Sometimes, lining a pan with smooth brown wrapping paper, waxed paper or parchment is recommended.

Sift and measure the dry ingredients. Although they are usually added to the batter last, they should be prepared first because once the eggs are beaten, the cake should get into the oven as quickly as possible. Usu-

Electric mixer. A mixer with special attachments is an inestimable aid to cake bakers. It should be strong enough to cream butter and beat heavy batters and, ideally, should be equipped with wire whisk and dough hook attachments to, respectively, beat volume into eggs and knead yeast dough until smooth.

Mary Ann, springform and layer cake pans. A Mary Ann pan produces a cake with a central depression that is meant to be filled with fruit, while a springform, with sides that spring free of a cake, is a necessity for delicate cheesecakes and tortes; and sturdy layer cake pans are an all-purpose cake-baking necessity.

Kugelhopf, angel food and plain tubed pan. As shown here, there is more than one type of tubed cake pan. A fluted one is traditional for a yeast-raised *Kugelhopf*; a pan with an extra-long, narrow tube and removable bottom is essential for an angel food cake; and a plain tubed pan is useful for fruit and other cakes.

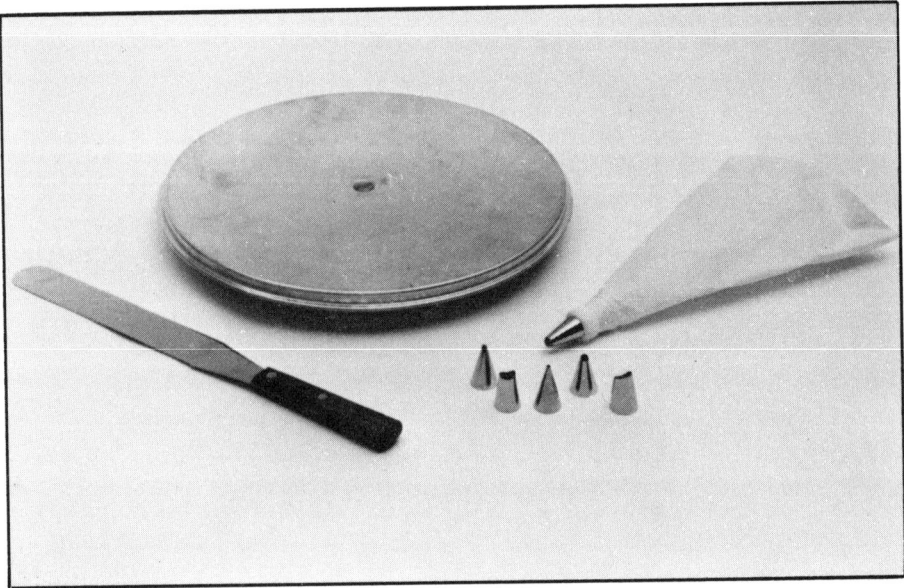

Turntable, spatula and decorating set. A turntable makes all sides of a cake easily accessible for frosting and decorating. To frost a cake smoothly, a long, flexible metal spatula is best, and a small pastry bag with a set of decorating tips is used to embellish a cake with delicate stars, rosettes, ribbons or calligraphy.

ally a recipe calls for sifting the flour before measuring; then it is re-sifted with the other dry ingredients—baking powder, soda, spices or cocoa—so they are all evenly distributed in the flour. Once the flour is in the batter, do as little stirring as possible.

Mixing the Batter. Mixing can begin once the oven is heated; the ingredients are sifted, measured and at room temperature; and the pans are ready and waiting on the countertop. It may require a variety of motions: creaming, stirring, beating, whipping and maybe even kneading. Mastering these techniques is important.

To cream butter and sugar, beat them together with the back of a wooden spoon against the side of the bowl in short, rocking strokes until the mixture is light and fluffy. Or, with an electric mixer, beat at medium speed about three minutes. When creaming, don't overbeat, or the butter will separate, become oily and give the cake a coarse texture.

Stirring is simply the mixing of ingredients together in a rotary motion with a wooden spoon. Its purpose is only to incorporate ingredients into the batter; it should stop once the ingredients are combined.

Beating, the more vigorous version of stirring, introduces air into batter and activates the gluten in flour. It can ruin the texture of a delicate cake, so beat only when the recipe says to. If a recipe calls for beaten egg whites, beat them in a warm (not hot, not cool, just warm), clean, grease-free bowl with grease-free beaters. To be sure the equipment is grease-free, wipe it with lemon juice or vinegar, rinse in water, and dry with paper towels. The classic tools for beating egg whites are a copper bowl and a thin, flexible, many-stranded wire whisk; but a stainless-steel or other non-aluminum metal bowl and an electric mixer may also be used. Begin beating slowly. When the whites are foamy, some cooks throw in a pinch of cream of tartar to help things along (this is unnecessary in a copper bowl). Then accelerate the beating, keeping the whole mass of whites in constant motion. When they're ready, they'll stick to the bowl when it's turned upside down. They should still be shiny. Overbeaten whites turn dull and break up into pieces; they will collapse in the oven and take the cake down with them. Overbeaten whites can be rescued, however, by adding an unbeaten egg white and beating them again. When the shiny peaks are restored, stop.

Folding is a method by which ingredients are combined as quickly as possible without beating. It is generally used for beaten or whipped ingredients like eggs and heavy cream, whose airiness needs to be preserved. For example, to incorporate beaten egg whites into a heavier batter, mix a bit of the whites into the batter to lighten it. Then put the rest of the whites on top of the lightened batter mixture. With a rubber spatula (some cooks prefer the direct contact method and use their hands, fingers spread, instead), slice down through the center of the mixture, then follow along the bottom and up the side of the bowl and over the top to make a complete circular motion, turning the container slowly with the other hand. Continue, slowly and gently, until no large patches of egg white are visible. To combine dry with whipped ingredients, sprinkle the dry ones on top and then gently fold them in.

Kneading may be required for cakes made with yeast, like *panettone* or *Stollen*. Fold the dough toward you, then press it away from you with the heel of your hand. Give it a slight turn, then fold and press again. Repeat until the dough is smooth, elastic and satiny. Soft doughs, like that used for making *baba*, are very sticky at first and require hard working in a bowl. Slap the dough against the bowl and stretch it by lifting and letting the strands fall back into it. When the dough becomes less sticky, knead it on a flat surface until air blisters appear at the surface.

Baking. As soon as the batter has received the final touches, pour it gently into the pan(s) and pop it into the oven immediately. In the oven, spacing is critical. If the oven is crowded, and the cake pans touch the sides or one another, the air won't circulate properly and the cake is likely to rise unevenly. The middle rack is best for layer and sponge cakes; the bottom rack, where temperatures are lower, is best for angel food and fruit cakes. To prevent the cake from burning, do not use the top rack, where the oven is hottest.

Cooking times are not to be trusted. When a cake smells done, take a look, but not before. If it's light brown and has pulled away from the sides of the pan, it may well be ready. There are two tests for doneness. When pressed lightly with a fingertip, most done cakes will spring back. But rich cakes and chocolate cakes may dent slightly even when fully baked. A second test is to insert a wire cake tester or toothpick into the center of the cake. If the cake is done, the tester will emerge perfectly clean. Chocolate cakes have a tendency to burn and should get particularly close attention as the cooking time nears its end.

When a cake is done, it must be allowed to cool. Cakes made with shortening may be left in the pan on a rack for five to ten minutes, then loosened with a spatula and inverted onto the rack. A sponge cake should be inverted in the pan on a rack (a tube pan may be hung on a bottle) until it is completely cool.

Decorating. Decorating can vary from the simplest sprinkling of powdered sugar to intricate designs of molded garlands and flowers. Whipped cream frostings and fillings, crunchy nuts, creamy slivers of chocolate or plump fresh berries will complement the cake's flavors and texture while adding visual appeal.

Fluffy boiled icings are made by pouring a hot sugar syrup, cooked to the soft ball stage (238 F.) in a thin stream over egg whites while beating them. Other cooked frostings are also cooked to the soft or hard ball stage. If the icing is too thick, add a little boiling water; if too thin, beat it over a pan of boiling water, always making sure it is the right consistency before putting it on the cake.

Uncooked icings usually depend on butter and the cornstarch in powdered sugar for their consistency. The simplest is merely a glaze of powdered sugar and a liquid; richer icings add butter and egg yolks. An electric beater is a great help in dealing with the heavy mixtures. Frostings with a high butter content freeze well. They may be kept in the freezer several weeks. After thawing a butter icing, beat it to the right consistency for spreading.

Whipped cream makes a light, tasty filling or topping for many cakes. You'll want a balloon whip or a hand-held electric mixer and a well-chilled glass, metal or porcelain bowl. Use a circular, whipping motion, and as the cream begins to thicken, add flavoring and sugar. Continue to beat until the cream forms stiff, fluffy peaks. If the cake is not to be served right away, put the cream in a fine-meshed sieve or a sieve lined with cheesecloth and set it over a bowl in the refrigerator. This will allow any liquid in the cream to drain off. Spread the cream on the cake just before serving.

Some glazes are added while the cake is still warm, but most icings and frostings require a cool cake. First, make sure the cake is symmetrical by trimming off any uneven edges with a knife. To split a torte in two layers, measure the height with a ruler and mark the midpoint all around with toothpicks as guides to follow when slicing through the cake with a long, sharp knife. The same ruler and toothpick method will help in cutting a sheet cake into petit fours.

For those who bake frequently, a decorating turntable is also a good investment. After the cake is frosted, it can be transferred to a serving platter with one or two long, wide, heavy spatulas. If you don't have a turntable, put the cake on a serving plate and slip four strips of waxed paper under the edges to keep the plate clean. Remove the strips after the cake is frosted. The best tool for spreading frosting or filling is a long, thin, flexible metal spatula.

Once the frosting has been spread and has hardened, more decorations can be added with a pastry bag. Fill the pastry bag only two-thirds full with more frosting or whipped cream. Twist the top tight, squeeze with one hand, and guide with the other. Even a simple butter cream frosting border around the top edge of a layer cake will give it a neat, professional touch. With different metal tubes, stars, fluted ribbons, flowers and leaves are possible. For fine writing, a decorating "pen" is available.

Storage. Most cakes will keep several days in cake keepers, but cakes with custard or whipped cream frostings must be refrigerated. Fruit cake will keep indefinitely—as long as 25 years!—if buried in powdered sugar and placed in a tightly covered tin. Cake batter cannot be frozen, nor can cakes with custard or fruit fillings. Fluffy frostings made with egg white don't freeze well either. Cakes with butter frostings, however, may be frozen for up to two months. Put them in the freezer unwrapped, and when frozen, wrap them airtight in freezer wrap or aluminum foil. To prevent crushing, place them in a box. Unwrap them as soon as they're removed from the freezer. Un-iced cakes also freeze well and keep for three to four months. They should be wrapped before freezing and left in their wrappings while they thaw. Because defrosted cakes dry out quickly, they should be left frozen until ready to use.

Coffee and Tea Cakes

KUGLOF

George and Arthur Herbst

2 large cakes

2 OUNCES COMPRESSED YEAST
⅓ POUND (⅔ CUP) SUGAR
2½ CUPS MILK
3 EGGS
2 POUNDS (ABOUT 8 CUPS) ALL-PURPOSE FLOUR, APPROXIMATELY

4 TEASPOONS SALT
2 TEASPOONS VANILLA EXTRACT
3½ STICKS UNSALTED BUTTER
1½ TEASPOONS GROUND CINNAMON
½ CUP SUGAR
2 CUPS RAISINS

1. Cream the yeast and sugar together in a mixer.
2. With the machine running, add the milk in a thin stream. Next, add the eggs, one at a time.
3. If you have a mixer with a dough hook, fit it on the machine and, with the machine running, sprinkle enough flour into the yeast mixture to form a soft dough. Add the salt and vanilla. Then knead in more flour until the dough is smooth and elastic and leaves the sides of the bowl and the dough hook clean. Turn the dough onto a table, cover it with a clean towel and allow it to rest for 30 minutes.

   Note: If you do not have an electric mixer with a dough hook attachment, combine the ingredients in the same order in a bowl to form a soft dough; then knead the dough by hand on a good work surface until it is smooth and elastic. Incorporate more flour as necessary to prevent the dough from sticking. When the dough is ready, cover it with a towel and let it rest for 30 minutes.

4. Soften the butter in the mixer or knead it by hand, until it is somewhat malleable but still quite cold. Pinch off bits of the butter and roll it into the dough with a rolling pin, folding and turning as necessary. The butter should remain in lumps in the dough.
5. When all of the butter has been incorporated, roll the dough once more. Cover and place it in the refrigerator to rest for 30 minutes.
6. Remove the dough from the refrigerator and roll it again, folding and turning, until it is almost completely homogeneous. Only tiny flecks of butter should remain visible.
7. Divide the dough into two equal parts and roll each into a 18" x 12" rectangle.
8. Combine the cinnamon and sugar. Sprinkle each rectangle of dough with half

of the cinnamon-sugar mixture and half of the raisins. Then roll each rectangle into a cylinder, starting from the long side.

9. Butter the insides of two 9'' to 10'' *kuglof* pans. Then twist a cylinder of dough around the tube of each pan and pinch the ends together. Allow the dough to rise in a warm place until it has doubled in bulk, approximately 1 hour.
10. Preheat the oven to 375 F.
11. Bake the *kuglofs* for about an hour, or until a cake tester inserted in the middle comes out clean.
12. Remove the cakes from their pans almost immediately and cool them on a wire rack.

Note: You may sprinkle powdered sugar over the cake before serving it. And slivered almonds may be added to the cake, if you like. For another variation, a sprinkling of cocoa powder and sugar may be substituted for the cinnamon, sugar and raisin filling. Leftover *kuglof* is excellent toasted and buttered.

APPLE COFFEE CAKE

Carol Cutler

One 8'' x 4'' loaf cake

½ POUND (2 TO 3) TART APPLES
8 TABLESPOONS (1 STICK) BUTTER
2 EGGS
1 CUP SUGAR
2 TABLESPOONS BUTTERMILK OR
   SOUR MILK
1 TEASPOON VANILLA EXTRACT
½ TEASPOON CINNAMON
¼ TEASPOON NUTMEG
¼ TEASPOON SALT
2 TEASPOONS BAKING POWDER
½ TEASPOON BAKING SODA
2 CUPS FLOUR

1. Preheat the oven to 350 F.
2. Peel, quarter, core and grate the apples.
3. In a heavy skillet, melt the butter and add the apples, turning them over and over to coat thoroughly with the butter. Simmer for 30 seconds and take off the heat at once. Set aside.
4. Beat together the eggs and sugar; then add the milk, vanilla, cinnamon, nutmeg, salt, baking powder and baking soda and mix well. Add the flour slowly and beat thoroughly. Fold in the apples and melted butter.
5. Grease and flour a 8¼'' x 4½'' x 2½''-deep loaf pan and pour in the batter. Bake in the hot oven for 50 to 55 minutes, or until the top surface cracks and a toothpick plunged in the center comes out clean. Remove from the pan while still slightly warm.
6. The cake can be served while fresh, or refrigerated; it will keep very well in the refrigerator and freezes perfectly.

Note: Nuts may be added to the batter for a richer loaf.

PANETTONE

Nicola Zanghi

1 large cake

This is the traditional Italian coffee cake served during the winter holiday season. It goes as well with white wine and champagne as it does with coffee.

1 PACKAGE ACTIVE DRY YEAST
1 CUP WARMED MILK
1½ POUNDS (ABOUT 5¼ CUPS) FLOUR, SIFTED
1 TEASPOON SALT
2 TABLESPOONS SUGAR
8 TABLESPOONS (1 STICK) UNSALTED BUTTER
4 LARGE EGGS, AT ROOM TEMPERATURE
GRATED RIND OF ½ ORANGE
GRATED RIND OF ½ LEMON
1 TEASPOON VANILLA EXTRACT
1 CUP CANDIED FRUITS, STEEPED OVERNIGHT IN RUM*
½ CUP RAISINS, STEEPED OVERNIGHT IN RUM*

1. Dissolve the yeast in the warm milk, then stir the mixture into 1 pound (3½ cups) of the flour. Work into a dough. Put the dough in a bowl, place in a warm area and let rise for 2 hours.

2. Combine the salt, sugar, butter, eggs, orange and lemon rind, vanilla, candied fruit and raisins (with the rum) and the remaining flour and work together into a dough-like consistency.

3. Knead this mixture into the yeast and flour dough after it has risen, and refrigerate the dough overnight.

   Note: Care should be taken not to overwork the dough lest it become tough and chewy.

4. Preheat the oven to 375 F.

5. Transfer the dough from the mixing bowl to a buttered 6- to 8-cup tubeless *Kugelhopf*, charlotte or dome-shaped mold. Do not punch down or knead the dough.

6. Bake for 35 minutes in the preheated oven, or until the cake springs back when gently pressed in the center.

* Steep the fruits in glass measuring cups with just enough rum to cover.

HONEY AND SPICE CAKES (LES NONNETTES)

Mireille Johnston

12 small cakes

These delicious little honey and spice cakes are filled with warm apricot jam or marmalade. The recipe originated in the convents of Burgundy, as early as the 14th Century (hence the name *nonnettes*, which means little nuns).

1 CUP HONEY, AS FRAGRANT AS
   POSSIBLE
½ CUP WARM WATER
½ CUP SUGAR
¼ TEASPOON SALT
1½ TEASPOONS BAKING SODA
2 CUPS RYE FLOUR (AVAILABLE IN
   HEALTH FOOD STORES AND MANY
   SUPERMARKETS)
½ CUP UNBLANCHED, GROUND OR
   CHOPPED ALMONDS
¼ CUP GOOD DARK RUM
2 TEASPOONS ANISE POWDER OR
   ANISE SEEDS
⅛ TEASPOON CINNAMON
⅛ TEASPOON GROUND CLOVES
½ CUP *GLACÉED* FRUIT OR MALAGA
   RAISINS
¾ CUP (12 TABLESPOONS) APRICOT
   JAM OR ORANGE MARMALADE, AS
   TART AS POSSIBLE
¼ CUP CONFECTIONERS' SUGAR

1. Preheat the oven to 325 F.
2. Put the honey, warm water and sugar in a large bowl and stir well.
3. Add the salt, soda and flour and beat vigorously for 5 minutes (you can use an electric blender or food processor for this step).
4. Stir in the ground or chopped almonds, rum, spices and fruit, blending well.
5. Pour the mixture into a well-buttered, 12-cup muffin tin, filling each cup two-thirds full. Bake for about 25 minutes, or until a knife or skewer plunged in the center of a cake comes out clean.
6. Remove the cakes from the oven and let them cool in the pan for 15 minutes; then unmold them onto a cake rack to finish cooling.
7. Meanwhile, place the tart apricot jam or orange marmalade in a small saucepan and warm over low heat.
8. When the *nonnettes* are cold, slice them in half horizontally and spread a tablespoon of warm jam over the cut surfaces of each cake. Fit the halves back together and sprinkle the cakes with confectioners' sugar.

Note: The flavor of the *nonnettes* improves if they are wrapped in foil and kept several days before eating.

MADELEINES

Raymond Sokolov

3½ to 4 dozen

4 EGGS, AT ROOM TEMPERATURE
¼ TEASPOON SALT
⅔ CUP SUGAR
1 TEASPOON VANILLA EXTRACT
1 CUP SIFTED FLOUR
8 TABLESPOONS (1 STICK) BUTTER,
   MELTED AND COOLED

1. Place the racks near the bottom of the oven. Preheat the oven to 400 F.
2. Grease well and flour the pans for 4 dozen madeleines.

Continued from preceding page

Note: If only half this many pans are available, cut the recipe in half and make the second batch after the first one is completed. If you don't do this, the butter, on standing, settles to the bottom and causes a heavy rough layer.

3. Beat the eggs with the salt, adding the sugar gradually, until the mixture has increased considerably in volume and is very pale and thick. Stir in the vanilla.
4. Sift about ¼ of the flour at a time over the egg mixture and fold it in until no flour shows.
5. Add the butter about a tablespoon at a time and fold it in as quickly as possible.
6. Fill the prepared pans about ¾ full, place in the oven immediately, and bake until the cakes are golden brown, about 10 minutes.

BURNT SUGAR CUPCAKES

Ruth Ellen Church

18 to 24 cupcakes

These cupcakes come from an old-fashioned, old family recipe, characteristic of Midwestern cookery in the days when farm women made six or eight desserts for family gatherings: two or three kinds of cakes, several pies and hand-cranked ice cream.

Burnt Sugar Syrup:
½ CUP SUGAR
¼ CUP HOT WATER

Cupcakes:
3 CUPS SIFTED CAKE FLOUR
3 TEASPOONS BAKING POWDER
½ TEASPOON SALT

8 TABLESPOONS (1 STICK) BUTTER
1¼ CUPS SUGAR
3 EGGS, SEPARATED
1 CUP MILK
1 TEASPOON VANILLA EXTRACT
CONFECTIONERS' SUGAR OR A 7-MINUTE FROSTING

1. In a small, heavy, iron skillet, gently heat the sugar until it melts, stirring constantly with a wooden spoon.
2. When the syrup is a golden caramel color, remove it from the heat. Add the hot water and stir until the syrup has liquefied again. The hot water will cause the syrup to lump, but the stirring will smooth the lumps out. Allow to cool.
3. Preheat the oven to 375 F.
4. Sift together the flour, baking powder and salt. Set aside.
5. Cream the butter and sugar until fluffy and light in color.
6. Add the egg yolks, one at a time, and beat well after each addition.
7. Add the flour mixture and milk to the batter in alternate portions, beating well after each addition.
8. Add the vanilla and 2 tablespoons of the burnt sugar syrup. Stir well.

9. Whip the egg whites until they hold soft peaks and fold into the batter gently but thoroughly.
10. Spoon the batter into muffin pans that have been buttered or lined with paper cups, filling each not more than two-thirds full.
11. Bake in the preheated oven about 20 minutes, or until the cakes test done with a cake tester or wooden toothpick.
12. Meanwhile, make the frosting of your choice and flavor it with the remaining caramel syrup.
13. Let the cakes cool for 5 to 10 minutes in the pan, then place them on a rack to cool completely. Frost and serve.

SOUR CREAM COFFEE CAKE

Ruth Spear

One 10" cake

½ POUND (2 STICKS) BUTTER, SOFTENED
1½ CUPS SUGAR
3 EGGS
3 CUPS FLOUR
½ TEASPOON PLUS A PINCH OF SALT
1 TABLESPOON BAKING POWDER
1 TEASPOON BAKING SODA
1 CUP SOUR CREAM
1 TEASPOON VANILLA EXTRACT
½ CUP FIRMLY PACKED BROWN SUGAR
¾ CUP CHOPPED WALNUTS OR PECANS
2 TEASPOONS CINNAMON
1 HEAPING TEASPOON COCOA

1. Preheat the oven to 350 F.
2. Butter a 10" tube springform pan or an angel-food cake pan. Set aside.
3. Cream the butter with 1 cup of the sugar until light and fluffy. Beat in the eggs, one at a time.
4. Sift together the flour, ½ teaspoon of salt, baking powder and baking soda. Add to the batter, blending well. Mix in the sour cream and the vanilla.

   Note: If the batter appears too stiff, thin it with up to 4 tablespoons of milk.
5. In a small bowl, blend the remaining ½ cup sugar with the brown sugar, a pinch of salt, the nuts, cinnamon and cocoa. Set aside.
6. Pour half the batter into the pan and smooth it with a spatula. Sprinkle half the cinnamon-nut mixture over the batter in the pan. Add the remaining batter and sprinkle the top with the remaining cinnamon-nut mixture.
7. Bake in the preheated oven for 50 minutes.
8. Cool for 30 minutes in the tin. Then, remove the sides and ease off the bottom of the springform pan, or remove the angel-food tin, and place the cake on a rack to cool completely before cutting or storing.

LEMON GLAZED TEA CAKE

Emanuel and Madeline Greenberg

One 13" x 9" cake

1½ CUPS SIFTED ALL-PURPOSE FLOUR
1½ TEASPOONS BAKING POWDER
¼ TEASPOON SALT
6 TABLESPOONS (¾ STICK) BUTTER
  (PREFERABLY UNSALTED)
1 CUP SUGAR
2 EGGS, BEATEN

½ CUP MILK
GRATED RIND OF 1 LEMON

Glaze:
⅔ CUP SUGAR
JUICE OF 1 LEMON

1. Preheat the oven to 350 F.
2. Butter a 13" x 9" baking pan.
3. Sift together the flour, baking powder and salt. Set aside.
4. In a large mixing bowl, beat the butter until fluffy. Gradually beat in the sugar. Beat in the eggs, flour mixture, milk and lemon rind.
5. Pour the batter into the prepared pan and bake for 25 minutes.
6. While the cake is baking, combine the sugar and lemon juice for the glaze.
7. When the cake has been in the oven for 25 minutes, spoon the glaze mixture over the top of it and continue to bake for 5 minutes more.
8. While the cake is still warm, cut it into 1" squares. Place each square in a small paper baking cup.

Note: The cake may, of course, be cut into larger squares or bars, and it makes a good dessert.

ECCLES CAKES

Rona Deme

Twelve 4" cakes

8 OUNCES PUFF PASTRY
4 TABLESPOONS (½ STICK) BUTTER
¼ CUP SUGAR
2 OUNCES (ABOUT ½ CUP) SULTANAS
2 OUNCES (ABOUT ½ CUP) CURRANTS
2 OUNCES (ABOUT ½ CUP) CANDIED
  PEEL
GRATED RIND AND JUICE OF 1 LEMON
GOOD PINCH OF ALLSPICE
MILK
SUGAR

1. Preheat the oven to 400 F.

2. Roll the puff pastry to the thickness of a penny. Using a sharp-edged cutter, cut into approximately twelve 4" rounds.
3. Cream the butter and sugar together, then work in all the remaining ingredients, except the milk and sugar.
4. Place a spoonful of the mixture on one-half of each of the pastry circles. Fold each circle in half and press the edges together firmly.
5. Using a rolling pin and your fingers, carefully roll and stretch the semi-circle as close as possible back into a circular shape.
6. Make several slits on the top of each cake, brush with milk and sprinkle with a bit of sugar.
7. Place on a baking sheet and bake in the center of the oven for 25 minutes, or until golden brown.

RUM-RAISIN TEA LOAF

Elizabeth Schneider Colchie

1 loaf

12 TABLESPOONS (1½ STICKS) UNSALTED BUTTER, SOFTENED
⅔ CUP CAKE FLOUR
¾ CUP PLUS 1 TABLESPOON ALL-PURPOSE FLOUR
¼ TEASPOON GROUND MACE
¼ TEASPOON SALT
¼ CUP DARK RUM
3 LARGE EGGS, AT ROOM TEMPERATURE
¾ CUP SUGAR
¾ CUP GOLDEN RAISINS
½ TEASPOON BAKING POWDER

1. Preheat the oven to 350 F.
2. Grease and flour a 4- to 5-cup loaf pan.
3. In a medium-sized bowl, beat the butter with an electric mixer until very creamy.
4. Gradually sift in the cake flour, ¾ cup all-purpose flour, the mace and salt, beating on high speed; then, gradually add the rum, continuing on high speed.
5. In a small bowl and with clean beaters, beat the eggs with the sugar until very thick and pale and tripled in volume, about 8 to 12 minutes.
6. Return the bowl containing the butter to the mixer and, with the machine set at the lowest speed, add the egg mixture to the butter-flour mixture, about one-quarter at a time, beating just enough to barely combine.
7. Toss the raisins with the remaining tablespoon of flour and the baking powder and fold them into the batter gently, but distributing them as evenly as possible.
8. Turn the batter into the prepared pan and bake in the center of the preheated oven for 1 hour, or until the center of the cake tests done.
9. Cool the cake in the pan for 10 minutes, then run a knife around the edges and remove it from the pan. Cool completely on a rack.

Continued from preceding page

10. Wrap in plastic and keep at room temperature for at least 24 hours before serving.

BUTTERFLY CAKES

Rona Deme

2 dozen small cakes

½ CUP ALL-PURPOSE FLOUR
½ CUP CORNSTARCH
1 TEASPOON BAKING POWDER
PINCH OF SALT
4 EGGS, SEPARATED
½ CUP SUGAR
¼ CUP RASPBERRY JAM, APPROX-
   IMATELY
½ TO ¾ CUP WHIPPED CREAM,
   APPROXIMATELY
CONFECTIONERS' SUGAR

1. Preheat the oven to 400 F.
2. Butter or line with paper cups the smallest cake, bun or muffin tins you can find.
3. Sift together the flour, cornstarch, baking powder and salt.
4. Beat the egg whites until stiff and "peaky." Gradually beat in the sugar, until thick and smooth. Beat in the egg yolks. Carefully fold in the dry ingredients.
5. Divide the batter between the tins and bake in the preheated oven until golden brown, about 10 minutes. Allow to cool.
6. Cut a shallow cone shape out of the top of each cake. Put a small amount of jam in the bottom of each hole and top with a dollop of whipped cream. Place the cone-shaped cut-out back on top of the cream and dust with a little confectioners' sugar.

Fruit Cakes and Cakes with Fruit

DUNDEE CAKE

Rona Deme

One 7" cake

2 CUPS ALL-PURPOSE FLOUR
1½ TEASPOONS BAKING POWDER
1 TEASPOON GROUND ALLSPICE
1 POUND MIXED, DRIED FRUITS, SUCH AS RAISINS, CURRANTS, SULTANAS, DATES AND FIGS
2 OUNCES *GLACÉED* CHERRIES, FLOURED
1 OUNCE (ABOUT ¼ CUP) CANDIED LEMON PEEL
1 OUNCE (ABOUT ¼ CUP) CANDIED ORANGE PEEL
2 OUNCES (ABOUT ½ CUP) CHOPPED ALMONDS
12 TABLESPOONS (1½ STICKS) BUTTER
¾ CUP SUGAR
3 EGGS
1 TABLESPOON MOLASSES
2 TABLESPOONS MILK, APPROXIMATELY
¼ CUP RUM OR BRANDY (OPTIONAL)
2 OUNCES (ABOUT ½ CUP) SPLIT ALMONDS
1 EGG WHITE, LIGHTLY BEATEN

1. Preheat the oven to 325 F.
2. Butter and flour a 7"-round, 3"-deep cake tin. Set aside.
3. Sift together the flour, baking powder and allspice.
4. In a large bowl, combine the dried fruits, *glacéed* cherries, candied lemon and orange peels and chopped almonds and mix together well.
5. Cream the butter and sugar together until light and fluffy. Beat in the eggs, one at a time, then stir in the flour mixture.
6. Add the molasses and enough milk to make a batter of "slow-dropping consistency."
7. Add the fruit mixture and stir together until all the ingredients are well-coated with batter and evenly distributed.
8. For special occasions, stir in the rum or brandy.
9. Turn the batter into the buttered and floured tin and decorate the circumference of the cake with the split almonds. Brush with egg white to glaze and to make the almonds stick to the cake.
10. Bake in the preheated oven for 2 to 2½ hours, or until a toothpick or cake

Continued from preceding page

tester inserted in the center of the cake comes out clean. Cool in the tin.

Note: If the cake has been made with rum or brandy, it can be aged for 4 to 5 weeks. Douse once a week with several spoonfuls of the liquor and keep refrigerated or in a cool place.

DRESDNER STOLLEN

Bianca Brown

One 12"-long Stollen

½ CUP DICED, MIXED CANDIED FRUITS
¼ CUP SULTANAS
¼ CUP CURRANTS
2 TABLESPOONS DICED CANDIED CITRON
3 TABLESPOONS RUM
1 PACKAGE ACTIVE DRY YEAST
⅓ CUP PLUS 1 TEASPOON SUGAR
2 TABLESPOONS LUKEWARM WATER
⅓ CUP MILK
6 TABLESPOONS (¾ STICK) UNSALTED BUTTER
½ TEASPOON SALT
2¾ TO 3 CUPS ALL-PURPOSE FLOUR
1 EGG PLUS 1 EGG YOLK, LIGHTLY BEATEN
1 TEASPOON GRATED LEMON RIND
⅓ CUP CHOPPED, BLANCHED ALMONDS
4 TABLESPOONS (½ STICK) BUTTER, MELTED
CONFECTIONERS' SUGAR

1. In a bowl, combine the mixed fruits, sultanas, currants, citron and rum. Toss the fruits and let them stand for 1 hour. Drain well, reserving the liquid.

2. In a small bowl, proof the yeast with 1 teaspoon sugar in lukewarm water for 10 minutes.

3. In a saucepan, heat the milk with the butter, ⅓ cup sugar and the salt until the butter melts and the sugar dissolves. Let cool to lukewarm.

4. In a large bowl, combine 2½ cups flour with the milk mixture, the yeast and egg yolk, rum and lemon rind. Mix the ingredients well to form a dough.

5. Turn the dough onto a lightly floured board and knead for 10 minutes, adding 1 to 2 tablespoons flour, if necessary, to get a smooth and elastic dough.

6. Toss the candied fruits and the almonds with 1½ tablespoons flour. Knead into the dough a little at a time, until they are evenly distributed.

7. Place the dough in a large, buttered bowl and turn so that it is lightly coated with butter. Cover the bowl with a tea towel and let the dough rise in a warm place for 2 hours, or until doubled in bulk.

8. Turn the dough on a lightly floured board and punch it down with a lightly floured rolling pin. Roll it into a 12" x 8" oval.

9. Brush the dough with 2 tablespoons of the melted butter. Fold one side lengthwise over the center of the oval and press it down lightly. Fold in the other side, overlapping the first side by 1", and press the edge down.

10. Transfer the *Stollen*, seam-side down, to a buttered baking sheet, cover it lightly with a tea towel and let it rise in a warm place for 1½ hours, or until almost doubled in bulk.
11. Preheat the oven to 400 F.
12. Bake the *Stollen* for 10 minutes, reduce the heat to 350 F. and bake it for 25 to 30 minutes longer, or until it sounds hollow when tapped on the bottom.
13. Brush it with the remaining 2 tablespoons of melted butter and let it cool on a rack. When cool, sprinkle with confectioners' sugar.

BANANA UPSIDE-DOWN CAKE

Paul Rubinstein

One 9" to 10" cake

8 TABLESPOONS (1 STICK) UNSALTED BUTTER, MELTED
2 CUPS BROWN SUGAR
2 TABLESPOONS DARK RUM
4 TO 6 JUST-RIPE BANANAS
4 EGGS, SEPARATED
1 CUP SUGAR
1 CUP ALL-PURPOSE FLOUR
1 TEASPOON DOUBLE-ACTING BAKING POWDER
⅛ TEASPOON SALT
SWEETENED WHIPPED CREAM (OPTIONAL)

1. Preheat the oven to 350 F.
2. In a bowl, combine the melted butter with the brown sugar and rum.
3. Over the bottom of a 9" to 10" (and at least 2" deep) heavy cast-iron or enameled, ovenproof skillet, spread an even layer of the rum-sugar mixture.
4. Peel and cut the bananas into ½"-thick slices. Arrange the banana slices over the surface of the butter-sugar-rum mixture so they are not quite touching one another.
5. With an electric mixer, beat the egg yolks and sugar together until the mixture is pale yellow and smooth.
6. Sift the flour and baking powder together into the yolk mixture and fold in thoroughly.
7. In a separate bowl, beat the egg whites with the salt until they form stiff peaks. Fold the beaten egg whites into the batter, just enough to distribute them well and eliminate any large pockets of white.
8. Pour this batter over the bananas in the skillet.
9. Bake in the preheated oven for 40 minutes, or until the cake has puffed up above the edges of the pan. Remove from the oven and place on a raised trivet or cooling rack for at least 15 minutes.
10. Holding the pan with a potholder, pass a sharp knife around the edges of the cake, then reverse it onto a serving platter or cake plate. The cake may be served warm, at room temperature or chilled. For added richness, accompany it with sweetened whipped cream.

STRAWBERRY MARY ANN

Susan Lipke

One 7" cake

A Mary Ann is a rather flat cake with an indentation in the middle destined to be filled with fruit. It is cooked in a special pan that is much like the fluted German *obsttortenform*.

Cake:
2 EGGS
¼ CUP SUGAR
¼ TEASPOON ALMOND EXTRACT
SEVERAL DROPS OF VANILLA EXTRACT
⅓ CUP CAKE FLOUR, MEASURED AFTER SIFTING
1½ TEASPOONS MELTED BUTTER

Filling:
2 TABLESPOONS SUGAR
1 TABLESPOON CORNSTARCH
2 EGG YOLKS
¼ TEASPOON ALMOND EXTRACT
SEVERAL DROPS OF VANILLA EXTRACT
½ CUP MILK
2 TABLESPOONS BLANCHED, SLICED ALMONDS
⅓ CUP HEAVY CREAM OR *CRÈME FRAÎCHE**, WHIPPED
½ TO ¾ PINT FRESH STRAWBERRIES, WASHED, HULLED AND THOROUGHLY DRIED

Currant Glaze:
½ CUP CURRANT JELLY
1 TABLESPOON SUGAR

1. Preheat the oven to 350 F.
2. Butter and flour a 7" Mary Ann pan.
3. In the bowl of an electric mixer, combine the eggs, sugar and almond and vanilla extracts. Set the bowl over almost boiling water and beat the egg mixture with a wire whisk until it is warm, about 15 to 20 seconds.
4. Fit the bowl onto the mixer and beat at high speed for 5 to 6 minutes, until the eggs are very pale and thick.
5. Very gently fold in the flour, a little at a time, then fold in the melted butter.
6. Turn the batter into the prepared pan and bake in the middle of the preheated oven for 20 to 25 minutes, until it is golden and springs back when pressed lightly with a fingertip.
7. Cool the cake in the pan, on a wire rack, then carefully unmold it.
8. While the cake is cooking, prepare the pastry cream. In a small bowl, combine the sugar, cornstarch, egg yolks and almond and vanilla extracts. Whisk together thoroughly.
9. In a small, heavy-bottomed saucepan, combine the milk and almonds and bring to a boil. Pour about half of the hot milk into the yolk mixture and whisk together until smooth.
10. Add the milk-yolk mixture to the rest of the milk in the pan and place over medium heat. Bring to a boil and cook, stirring constantly, for 1 to 2 minutes, until smooth.
11. Cover the surface of the cream with plastic wrap and refrigerate until well chilled, or beat the cream over ice until chilled.
12. An hour or so before assembling the cake, beat the chilled pastry cream for

a moment to loosen it, then fold in the whipped cream (or *crème fraîche*). Refrigerate for at least 30 minutes before assembling the cake.

13. Meanwhile, make the currant glaze. In a small saucepan, combine the currant jelly and sugar and boil together until thick and sticky, about 230 F. on a candy thermometer. Keep warm over hot water until ready to use.
14. Not more than an hour before serving, assemble the cake. Brush the indented area in the center of the cake with a little of the warm glaze, then spread two-thirds of the almond pastry cream over that.
15. Neatly arrange concentric circles of whole strawberries on top of the cream and brush them with the glaze.
16. Pipe the remaining cream through a pastry tube to make decorative rosettes around the edge of the cake and decorate with more almonds, if desired. Refrigerate until serving.

* To make your own *crème fraîche*, combine a pint of heavy cream with 1 tablespoon of buttermilk in a glass jar, cover and shake. Leave at room temperature until the cream thickens, from 5 or 6 to 24 hours, depending upon how warm the kitchen is. Shake the jar again, then refrigerate.

CHOCOLATE DATE CAKE

Paula J. Buchholz

One 9" x 13" cake

2 CUPS DICED FRESH DATES
1 CUP BOILING WATER
1 TEASPOON BAKING SODA
8 TABLESPOONS (1 STICK) BUTTER OR MARGARINE
1 CUP SUGAR
2 EGGS
1 TABLESPOON COCOA

1½ CUPS FLOUR
1 OUNCE UNSWEETENED CHOCOLATE
1 BAR (ABOUT 8 OUNCES) SEMISWEET OR SWEET CHOCOLATE
½ CUP (ABOUT 2½ OUNCES) DICED WALNUTS
CONFECTIONERS' SUGAR

1. Preheat the oven to 350 F.
2. Butter and flour a 9" x 13" pan.
3. Cover the dates with the boiling water. Allow the mixture to cool, then stir in the baking soda.
4. Cream together the butter or shortening and sugar until light and fluffy. Beat in the eggs, then stir in the cocoa and flour. Beat in the date mixture.
5. Pour the batter into the prepared pan.
6. Place the unsweetened chocolate, semisweet chocolate and nuts in the container of a food processor or blender. Give the machine a few quick on and off turns until the chocolate and nuts are coarsely grated. Sprinkle over the cake batter.
7. Bake in the preheated oven for 30 minutes.
8. Sprinkle the cake with confectioners' sugar and cut it into squares to serve.

BLUEBERRY CHEESECAKE

Linda Lewis

One 10" cake

With whole blueberries baked into the batter and served with a cold blueberry sauce, this delicious cake is a beauty to behold.

Crust:
8 TABLESPOONS (1 STICK) LIGHTLY SALTED BUTTER
1 CUP GRAHAM CRACKER CRUMBS
1 CUP FINELY GROUND PECANS OR WALNUTS
½ CUP SUGAR

Blueberry Cheese Filling:
6 EGGS, SEPARATED
1 CUP SUGAR
2 POUNDS RICOTTA CHEESE
¼ CUP HEAVY CREAM
½ CUP PLUS 2 TABLESPOONS ALL-PURPOSE FLOUR
1 SCANT TEASPOON GRATED LEMON RIND
2 CANS (15 OUNCES EACH) BLUEBERRIES IN HEAVY SYRUP
$1/8$ TEASPOON SALT

Blueberry Sauce:
2 TABLESPOONS CORNSTARCH
1 CUP SUGAR
2 TEASPOONS FRESHLY SQUEEZED LEMON JUICE
1 CUP SOUR CREAM
½ TEASPOON FRESHLY GRATED LEMON RIND
CONFECTIONERS' SUGAR

1. Place a rack in the center of the oven. Preheat the oven to 325 F.
2. Butter a 10" springform pan.
3. In a small saucepan, melt the butter and heat it until it turns a golden brown. In a large mixing bowl, combine the graham cracker crumbs, ground nuts and sugar. Add the melted butter and mix with a kitchen fork, blending thoroughly.
4. Using your fingers, press the buttered crumbs smoothly and firmly around the sides and bottom of the springform pan forming an $1/8$"-thick layer that rises approximately 2" up the sides.
5. In a large bowl of an electric mixer, beat the egg yolks with the sugar until thick. Add the ricotta cheese and mix thoroughly, then blend in the heavy cream, 4 tablespoons of the flour and the lemon rind. Beat until the mixture is thick and smooth.
6. Drain the blueberries and reserve the syrup. Place the drained blueberries in a small bowl and sift the remaining 6 tablespoons of flour over them. Toss the blueberries gently with your fingers, being careful not to crush them.

   Note: I have found that when the berries are coated with flour in this way, they will remain suspended throughout the batter rather than sinking to the bottom, as happens in conventional cheesecakes.

7. In a large metal bowl, beat the egg whites with a wire whisk until foamy; add the salt and continue to beat until they form soft peaks.
8. Using a rubber spatula, fold the egg whites into the cheese batter. When they are thoroughly blended, gently fold in the blueberries.
9. Pour the batter into the prepared springform pan and bake 50 to 60 minutes. The top of the cake should be lightly browned and feel firm when gently touched. Cool 1 hour before refrigerating. Refrigerate 6 hours before serving.

10. In a small bowl, dissolve the cornstarch in ¼ cup of the reserved blueberry syrup.
11. In a medium-sized saucepan, combine 1¾ cups blueberry syrup and the sugar over high heat. Bring to a boil, stirring constantly. Add the blueberry-cornstarch mixture and cook for 2 minutes. Stir in the lemon juice; remove from the heat and cool.
12. Blend in the sour cream and grated lemon rind. Refrigerate until ready to serve.
13. When ready to serve, remove the cheesecake from the springform pan, as follows. Run the blade of a thin, sharp knife around the edge of the pan, between the springform ring and the crust. Release the clip on the side of the pan and carefully lift off the ring. Place the cake, pan bottom and all, on a decorative serving platter and dust lightly with confectioners' sugar sifted through a fine sieve. Pass the chilled blueberry sauce in a separate bowl.

PEAR KUCHEN

Elizabeth Schneider Colchie

4 to 6 servings

1 CUP ALL-PURPOSE FLOUR
6 TO 8 TABLESPOONS SUGAR*
1 TEASPOON DOUBLE-ACTING BAKING POWDER
1 TEASPOON GROUND CARDAMOM
¼ TEASPOON SALT
⅛ TEASPOON FRESHLY GRATED NUTMEG
½ TEASPOON GRATED LEMON RIND
2 TABLESPOONS COLD BUTTER, CUT INTO SMALL PIECES
¼ CUP LIGHT CREAM OR HALF-AND-HALF
1 LARGE EGG
2 MEDIUM-LARGE, HARD-RIPE PEARS
2 TABLESPOONS MELTED BUTTER
⅓ CUP CHOPPED OR SLIVERED ALMONDS

1. Preheat the oven to 375 F.
2. Butter a 6" x 10" x 2" baking dish.
3. Into a bowl, sift together the flour, 3 tablespoons of the sugar, the baking powder, cardamom, salt and nutmeg. Stir in the lemon rind.
4. With a pastry blender, cut in the butter to form tiny, even particles.
5. In a cup, blend together the cream and egg and add this to the dry ingredients, mixing until the ingredients are just combined.
6. Spread the batter in the prepared baking dish.
7. Peel the pears, cut them into quarters and core them. Cut the quarters into very thin slices, about 4 to 5 per quarter.
8. Closely overlap the pear slices on the batter, forming two long rows.
9. Brush with the melted butter and sprinkle with the remaining 3 to 5 tablespoons

Continued from preceding page

of sugar. Sprinkle on the almonds.

10. Cover with foil and bake in the upper third of the preheated oven for 15 minutes. Remove the foil and bake 20 minutes more, or until the pears are lightly browned.
11. Let cool slightly and serve for breakfast or tea with slightly sweetened sour cream.

* Use 6 tablespoons of sugar if the pears are sweet.

SIMNEL CAKE

Maurice Moore-Betty

One 8" to 10" cake

½ POUND (2 STICKS) BUTTER
½ POUND (ABOUT 2 CUPS) SUGAR
6 EGGS
¾ POUND (ABOUT 3 CUPS) ALL-PURPOSE FLOUR
1 TEASPOON BAKING POWDER
½ POUND (ABOUT 1 CUP) GOLDEN RAISINS
6 OUNCES (ABOUT 6 TABLESPOONS) CURRANTS
2 OUNCES CANDIED LEMON PEEL, CHOPPED
1 TEASPOON GROUND ALLSPICE
¾ POUND ALMOND PASTE

1. Preheat the oven to 350 F.
2. In a mixer, cream the butter and sugar together. Add the eggs, one at a time, beating well after each addition.
3. Sift together the flour and baking powder. Dust the fruit and candied peel with a little of the flour to keep them from sticking together.
4. Stir the flour and fruits into the batter, along with the spices.
5. Line an 8"- to 10"-round cake pan with parchment paper. Spoon half of the cake mixture into the tin. Roll out three-quarters of the almond paste to the same diameter as the cake pan. It should be about ¾" thick. Lay it on top of the batter. Spoon the rest of the batter on top of the paste, and spread evenly.
6. Bake for approximately 3 hours in the preheated oven.
7. Roll out the remaining quarter of the almond paste and make a strip to fit around the top edge of the cake. Remove the cake from the oven, place the strip around the top of the cake and rough it up with a fork.
8. Return the cake to the oven and bake 30 minutes longer. Test for doneness.
9. Partially cool the cake in the pan, then remove to a rack to cool completely.

Note: Simnel cake will keep very well in an airtight container.

TRIFLE

Rona Deme

6 to 10 servings

24 LADYFINGERS, SPLIT IN HALF LENGTHWISE
3 BOXES BLACK RASPBERRY GELATIN
6 CUPS HOT WATER
RASPBERRY JAM
SHERRY OR COGNAC
1 CAN (8 OUNCES) UNSWEETENED PINEAPPLE BITS, DRAINED
3 LARGE, RIPE BANANAS, SLICED

Custard*:
½ CUP CORNSTARCH
PINCH OF SALT
½ CUP SUGAR (OR MORE, TO TASTE)
ONE 2"-LONG PIECE OF VANILLA BEAN, OR 2 TEASPOONS VANILLA EXTRACT
4 CUPS MILK
6 EGG YOLKS, LIGHTLY BEATEN

Garnish:
2 CUPS HEAVY CREAM, WHIPPED WITH 1 TABLESPOON SUGAR
BLANCHED ALMONDS. SLICED
GLACÉED CHERRIES, CUT INTO LITTLE PIECES

1. Line the bottom and sides of a 12"-square x 6"-deep dish (or a round dish of equivalent capacity) with ladyfingers.
2. Dissolve the gelatin in the hot water. Set aside to cool.
3. With a teaspoon, dribble small amounts of the raspberry jam over the bottom layer of the ladyfingers and then sprinkle with sherry (or cognac).
4. Spoon about a third of the cooled, but still liquid, gelatin over all of the ladyfingers, on both bottom and sides.
5. Spread a layer of drained pineapple bits over the bottom, followed by a layer of sliced banana.
6. Add another layer of the gelatin and refrigerate.
7. While the cake is chilling, prepare the custard. In a heavy saucepan, combine the cornstarch, salt, sugar, vanilla bean, if using it (do not add the vanilla extract at this point), and milk and stir until smooth.
8. Cook over low heat until the mixture thickens.
9. Add ½ cup of the thickened mixture to the egg yolks, blend and return this combined mixture to the saucepan. Cook over low heat for 5 to 8 minutes, stirring all the while. Remove the vanilla bean, if you have used one; or, if using vanilla extract, stir it in at this point. Set the custard aside to cool.
10. Cover the jelled trifle mixture with about a third of the cooled custard. Then cover the custard with more ladyfingers, jam, a sprinkle of sherry (or cognac), the pineapple, banana and some of the gelatin.
11. Make two more layers each of ladyfingers, gelatin and then covered with custard. Cover with waxed paper and refrigerate overnight.
12. To serve, top with dollops of whipped cream and sprinkle with the almonds and chopped *glacéed* cherries.

* Two standard-sized boxes of vanilla pudding mix may be substituted for the custard.

Tortes, Layer and Tube Cakes

SUPER LUCIOUS CHOCOLATE CAKE

Linda Lewis

One 9" layer cake

This cake is for chocolate addicts only! Rich and moist, it is wonderful baked in two layers, filled with chocolate butter cream and covered with a dark chocolate glaze. It is also excellent baked in a single layer, cut into squares while still warm and served simply with lightly sweetened whipped cream.

Cake:
2 CUPS ALL-PURPOSE FLOUR
2 TEASPOONS BAKING POWDER
PINCH OF SALT
½ CUP VEGETABLE SHORTENING
2 CUPS SUGAR
2 EGGS
½ CUP UNSWEETENED COCOA
2 TEASPOONS BAKING SODA
2 CUPS BOILING WATER
2 TEASPOONS VANILLA EXTRACT

Chocolate Butter Cream:
½ CUP WATER
½ CUP SUPERFINE SUGAR
5 EGG YOLKS
½ POUND (2 STICKS) UNSALTED BUTTER
3 OUNCES DARK, SWEET CHOCOLATE, MELTED AND COOLED

Dark Chocolate Glaze:
1 POUND SEMISWEET CHOCOLATE
1 CUP WATER
1 TEASPOON VANILLA EXTRACT

1. Have all the ingredients at room temperature.
2. Place a rack in the center of the oven, and preheat the oven to 350 F.
3. Grease two 9" layer cake pans. Cut waxed paper to line the pans and grease the waxed paper, as well. Lightly flour the pans and shake out any excess.
4. Sift the flour once, then resift it with the baking powder and salt. Set aside.
5. Cream the shortening in the large bowl of an electric mixer. Gradually add the sugar, beating until fluffy.
6. Add the eggs, one at a time, and beat until light and fluffy.
7. In a 1-quart measuring cup, combine the cocoa and the baking soda. Slowly add the boiling water, stirring until the mixture is thoroughly blended.
8. Add the flour to the sugar-egg mixture in fourths, alternating with the hot cocoa and mixing well after each addition. Add the vanilla.
9. Pour the batter into the prepared pans. (The batter is thin and will level itself.)

Bake for 25 to 30 minutes. When done, the tops of the cakes will spring back when pressed gently.

10. Set the cakes on a wire rack and let them cool completely before removing them from the pans.
11. Meanwhile, make the chocolate butter cream. In a small saucepan, combine the cup of water and sugar over medium-high heat and boil to the thread stage (236 F. on a candy thermometer).
12. In the large bowl of an electric mixer, beat the egg yolks until foamy.
13. With the machine running, add the hot sugar syrup to the egg yolks in a thin stream. Continue beating until the mixture is cool.
14. Beat in the butter, a tablespoon at a time.
15. Once all the butter has been added, blend in the chocolate. Set aside.

Note: If the butter cream is over-beaten and curdles, beat in a tablespoon of hot, melted butter. If the butter cream becomes too soft to spread, refrigerate it for 15 to 20 minutes. Any leftover butter cream can be kept in a tightly-sealed container in the refrigerator for a week, or may be frozen.

16. Next, make the chocolate glaze. Combine the chocolate and water in the top of a double boiler over simmering water.
17. Stir until smooth, shiny and well blended. Remove from the heat.
18. Stir in the vanilla, then cool to room temperature.
19. To assemble the cake, place one layer top-side down on a wire rack and spread it generously with a layer of the chocolate butter cream filling. Arrange the second layer on top of the butter cream, top-side up. Cover the entire cake, sides and top, with a thin film of butter cream.
20. Leaving the cake on the wire rack, refrigerate it for about 1 hour, or until the butter cream solidifies.
21. Remove the cake, still on the wire rack, from the refrigerator and place it over a jelly roll pan or baking sheet. Hold the pan of dark chocolate glaze several inches above the center of the cake and pour it evenly over the cake. If the glaze does not cover the cake evenly, simply scoop the excess glaze back into the pan and repeat the procedure. Smooth the glaze with a metal spatula, if necessary.

Note: Any leftover chocolate glaze may be stored in an airtight container in the refrigerator for a week. To reuse, simply melt in the top of a double boiler over simmering water. Also, it makes a delicious hot fudge sauce over ice cream.

22. When the glaze stops dripping, transfer the cake onto a serving plate, using two wide, stiff metal spatulas. Refrigerate until ready to serve.

Note: This recipe also makes a delicious sheet cake in a 13" x 9" x 1½" pan. Follow the same directions, but bake the cake for 30 to 35 minutes and then let it cool in the pan on a wire rack before cutting it into squares. Instead of butter cream and glaze, serve the cake topped with whipped cream.

DOBOS TORTE

Matt Kramer

One 9" layer cake

Jozsef C. Dobos created this torte. In 1906, Dobos donated his torte recipe to the Budapest Pastry and Honey-bread Makers' Guild to curtail the increasing number of bad imitations produced by competitors. The availability of the recipe enabled the world to enjoy authentic Dobos torte.

Cake:
7 EGGS, SEPARATED
3 EGG YOLKS
1 POUND (3½ CUPS) CONFECTIONERS' SUGAR, SIFTED
¾ CUP ALL-PURPOSE FLOUR, SIFTED

¾ POUND (3 STICKS) UNSALTED BUTTER, SOFTENED
5 EGG YOLKS
1 TEASPOON VANILLA EXTRACT
3 TABLESPOONS CONFECTIONERS' SUGAR

Filling:
¾ POUND BITTERSWEET CHOCOLATE (LINDT IS ESPECIALLY GOOD)

1. Preheat the oven to 400 F. and place the oven rack in the center of the oven.
2. Butter and flour the bottom of a 9" springform pan. Remove any excess flour by rapping the pan on a hard surface.

   Note: If you have more than one 9" pan bottom, do as many cake layers at one time as your oven allows.
3. Place the 10 egg yolks in a large bowl and beat with an electric mixer until they are thick and a pale lemon color.
4. Reduce the speed and add the sugar. Increase the speed to high again and beat for 5 minutes, or until very thick.
5. Add the flour, while continuing to beat, and beat for 5 more minutes. The resulting mixture will be extremely stiff.
6. Beat the 7 egg whites until stiff, but not dry. Incorporate the egg whites into the egg yolk mixture, gradually: First stir in a few spoonfuls of the beaten egg white; then fold in slightly larger amounts of the egg whites until the yolk mixture lightens; then gently fold in the balance of the whites.
7. With a large spoon or a small spatula, place a small amount of the batter on the prepared pan bottom. Smooth it evenly to the edges. The batter should be no more than ¼" thick.
8. Bake for 5 to 8 minutes, or until the top of the cake is golden brown (some dark spots may occur). Invert the cake on a rack, then quickly turn it right-side-up on a second rack to prevent the top side of the cake from sticking to the rack.
9. Repeat this process (buttering and flouring the pan each time) until you have seven layers of cake. Cooled layers may be placed on a clean, dry towel or between pieces of waxed paper, lightly sprinkled with confectioners' sugar.
10. To make the filling, melt the chocolate in a double boiler or over very low heat in a small, heavy saucepan. Stir until smooth and set it aside to cool completely.

11. In a large bowl of an electric mixer, cream the butter, add the egg yolks and vanilla and beat well.
12. Add the sugar and cooled chocolate. Beat thoroughly.
13. Spread a thin layer of chocolate on the top side of one layer of cake. Cover with a second layer of cake and spread it with some more chocolate filling. Repeat until all seven layers of cake have been used. Spread the remaining chocolate smoothly around the top and sides of the cake.
14. Refrigerate for at least 3 hours to set the icing.

Note: Dobos torte is traditionally topped with a layer of caramelized sugar. Not only is the sugar hard to work with, but it really doesn't taste very good. I prefer to top the cake with a layer of the chocolate filling instead. The torte will keep perfectly for several days and can be decently frozen.

ZUPPA INGLESE

Maria Luisa Scott and Jack Denton Scott

One 9" layer cake

½ CUP SUGAR
¼ CUP FLOUR
¼ TEASPOON SALT
2 CUPS HOT MILK
4 EGG YOLKS
½ TEASPOON VANILLA EXTRACT
2 TEASPOONS *CRÈME DE CACAO*

ONE 9" SPONGE CAKE, CUT INTO THREE ½"- TO ¾"-THICK LAYERS
⅔ CUP LIGHT RUM
1 CUP RASPBERRY JAM
1½ CUPS HEAVY CREAM, WHIPPED
CANDIED FRUIT
TOASTED ALMOND HALVES

1. In the top of a double boiler over boiling water, mix the sugar, flour and salt. Gradually stir in the hot milk and cook, stirring constantly, until thickened. Lower the heat.
2. In a bowl, beat the egg yolks. Gradually add part of the milk mixture to the yolks, stirring. Pour this mixture into the double boiler and cook over simmering water, stirring constantly, until very thick. Set aside to cool.
3. Divide the custard into two parts. Add the vanilla to one and the *crème de cacao* to the other. Mix the flavorings in well and chill.
4. Place one layer of the sponge cake on a large serving plate, sprinkle it with one-third of the rum. Spread the layer with half of the raspberry jam, then the vanilla custard.
5. Cover with a second layer of cake, sprinkle with one-third of the rum and spread with the remaining jam and the *crème de cacao*-flavored custard.
6. Set the third layer on top of the custard and sprinkle it with the remaining rum. Let it soak in well.
7. Just before serving, cover the top and sides of the cake with whipped cream and decorate with the candied fruit and the almond halves. Serve at room temperature.

YOGURT CHOCOLATE CAKE

Florence Fabricant

One large tube cake

Here is more proof that yogurt can be used in almost any recipe. This cake is moist and rich and stands up well to ice cream or whipped cream.

8 TABLESPOONS (1 STICK) BUTTER,
   SOFTENED
1½ CUPS SUGAR
2 EGGS
2 CUPS FLOUR
¾ CUP COCOA
1½ TEASPOONS BAKING SODA
1½ CUPS PLAIN YOGURT
1 TEASPOON VANILLA EXTRACT
CONFECTIONERS' SUGAR (OPTIONAL)

1. Preheat the oven to 350 F.
2. Butter and flour a 12-cup tube baking pan.
3. Cream the butter. Gradually add the sugar, and beat until the mixture is light and fluffy. Beat in the eggs, one at a time.
4. Sift the flour, cocoa and baking soda together and add to the batter in thirds, alternating with the yogurt. Stir in the vanilla.
5. Spread the batter in the prepared pan and bake until a cake tester comes out clean, about 50 minutes. Cool in the pan, set on a rack. When completely cool, invert the pan to remove the cake.
6. Serve it plain, or dusted with confectioners' sugar.

SWEET MOUTHFUL (BOCCONE DOLCE)

Matt Kramer

One 8" to 10" layer cake

4 EGG WHITES
PINCH OF SALT
¼ TEASPOON CREAM OF TARTAR
1⅓ CUPS SUPERFINE SUGAR*
4 CUPS HEAVY CREAM
2 PINTS FRESH STRAWBERRIES
6 OUNCES BITTERSWEET CHOCOLATE
   (PREFERABLY LINDT BITTERSWEET
   OR TOBLER EXTRA-BITTERSWEET)
3 TABLESPOONS COGNAC OR WATER

1. In a mixing bowl, beat the egg whites with the salt and cream of tartar until

they form soft, firm peaks.

2. Gradually add 1 cup of the sugar and continue to beat until the meringue is stiff and glossy.
3. Preheat the oven to 275 F.
4. Using an 8" to 10" springform pan base (or other circular shape) as a guide, cut three circles of waxed paper. Lightly oil both sides of the paper.
5. Place two of the circles on one baking sheet and the third circle on a second baking sheet. Spread the meringue about ¼" deep over each circle, as evenly as possible.
6. Bake the meringues for approximately 20 minutes, or until they are a very pale gold color and still pliable. Do not allow them to bake until they are stiff and crumbly. Peel the paper from the meringues and place them on racks to dry. (It won't peel easily.)
7. Whip the cream until thick. Gradually add the remaining ⅓ cup of sugar and beat until very stiff.
8. Wash the strawberries quickly under cold water and remove their green hulls. Reserve 1 pint of the strawberries, and slice the rest.
9. In a double boiler, or over very low direct heat in a small, heavy saucepan, melt the chocolate. Add the cognac or water, blend in and set aside to cool.
10. To assemble the cake, place a meringue layer on a serving plate and spread a thin layer of the melted chocolate over it. Then spread a ¾"-thick layer of the whipped cream over the chocolate. Cover the cream with an even layer of sliced strawberries.
11. Place a second layer of meringue over the strawberries, spread it first with chocolate, then with whipped cream and top with strawberries. Cover with the third layer of meringue.
12. Repeat the layers of chocolate, cream and sliced strawberries and then cover the top and sides of the cake with the remaining cream. Stud the top and sides of the finished cake with the whole strawberries.
13. Refrigerate for at least 2 hours before serving.

Note: An easy method of keeping the serving plate clean while constructing the cake is to cut four 1½"-wide strips of waxed paper and partly slide one under each side of the first meringue layer. The strips will form a square and should cover the serving plate all around the cake. When finished, just pull the strips out from under the cake and the plate should be fairly clean.

* The superfine granulation reduces the danger of gritty meringues and whipped cream.

WALNUT TORTE

Bianca Brown

One 9" layer cake

SHORTENING
6 EGGS, SEPARATED
½ CUP PLUS 2 TABLESPOONS SUGAR
1 OUNCE (1 SQUARE) SEMISWEET CHOCOLATE, GRATED
¼ TEASPOON INSTANT COFFEE (PREFERABLY *ESPRESSO*)
1½ TEASPOONS VANILLA EXTRACT
2 CUPS (½ POUND) COARSELY GROUND WALNUTS
⅓ CUP SIFTED DRY BREAD CRUMBS
PINCH OF SALT
1½ CUPS HEAVY CREAM
¼ CUP CONFECTIONERS' SUGAR
WALNUT HALVES OR CHOCOLATE CURLS

1. Preheat the oven to 350 F.
2. Dot the center of three 9" x 1½"-deep layer cake pans with shortening. Line each with a 9" round of waxed paper. It is not necessary to butter and flour the pans, although the cakes will be slightly easier to unmold if you do so.
3. In the bowl of an electric mixer, beat the egg yolks with ½ cup of sugar until thick and lemon colored. Beat in the chocolate.
4. Dissolve the instant coffee in 1 teaspoon of vanilla. Add to the bowl and beat in.
5. In a bowl, combine the ground walnuts with the bread crumbs.
6. In another bowl, beat the egg whites with the pinch of salt until they hold soft peaks. Gradually beat in 2 tablespoons of sugar, beating until the peaks are stiff but not dry.
7. Stir half of the nut mixture into the egg yolk mixture, then fold in one-third of the whites. Fold in the rest of the nut mixture and another third of the whites. Turn the entire mixture onto the remaining whites and fold them in lightly but thoroughly.
8. Divide the batter among the prepared cake pans, spreading it evenly. Bake the cakes in the preheated oven for 20 minutes, or until a cake tester inserted in the center comes out clean.
9. Transfer the pans to cake racks and let them cool for 20 minutes. With a sharply pointed knife, loosen the cake layers around the edges of the pans. Invert them onto the cake racks. Carefully remove the paper and let the cakes cool.
10. In a chilled bowl, beat the cream until it thickens slightly. Sift in the confectioners' sugar, add the remaining ½ teaspoon of vanilla and continue beating until the cream forms firm peaks when the beater is lifted.
11. To assemble the cake, spread one layer with one-fourth of the whipped cream, top it with a second layer and spread it, also, with one-fourth of the cream. Place the last layer on top and spread the top and the sides of the torte with the remaining cream. Decorate with walnut halves or chocolate curls.
12. Chill the cake for 1 hour before serving.

Note: The cake layers may be baked a day in advance.

ALMOND LAYER CAKE

Paul Rubinstein

One 9" layer cake

12 TABLESPOONS (1½ STICKS) UN-
  SALTED BUTTER, SOFTENED
6 EGGS
9 EGG YOLKS
3 TEASPOONS VANILLA EXTRACT
1 CUP PLUS 5 TABLESPOONS SUGAR
½ CUP FRESH OR CANNED ALMOND
  PASTE
1½ CUPS ALL-PURPOSE FLOUR
8 TABLESPOONS (1 STICK) UNSALTED
  BUTTER, MELTED
10 TABLESPOONS (1¼ STICKS) UN-
  SALTED BUTTER, CHILLED
2 TABLESPOONS RUM
1½ CUPS GROUND, TOASTED AL-
  MONDS (UNSALTED)

1. Preheat the oven to 350 F.
2. With 1 tablespoon of the softened butter, spread a thin coating on the inside surfaces of two 9" round, layer cake pans. Line the bottom of each pan with a round of waxed paper and spread another tablespoon of the softened butter on the paper rounds.
3. In a mixing bowl, combine the 6 whole eggs plus 2 of the yolks, 1 teaspoon of the vanilla and 1 cup of the sugar. Place the bowl over a saucepan of very hot, but not boiling, water to warm up for 10 minutes. Stir the eggs often to prevent them from cooking on the bottom.
4. Meanwhile, in another bowl, beat the almond paste with 2 of the remaining egg yolks until the combination is light and smooth. Set aside.
5. After the egg mixture has warmed for 10 minutes, beat it for several minutes longer with a hand-held electric mixer, until it is light and fluffy and achieves the texture of whipped cream.
6. Fold the almond paste into the egg mixture.
7. Sift the flour over the top of the egg mixture and fold it in gently but thoroughly. Slowly stir in the melted butter.
8. Pour the finished batter into the layer cake pans, dividing it evenly, and bake in the preheated oven for 18 to 20 minutes, until golden brown. Turn the cake layers out onto cooling racks and let stand while preparing the icing.
9. In a blender jar, place the remaining 5 egg yolks, 5 tablespoons of sugar and 2 teaspoons of vanilla. Run the blender at high speed, slowly adding the remaining 10 tablespoons of softened butter and then the 10 tablespoons of chilled butter, a little at a time. Add the rum.
10. Turn off the blender, scrape the icing into a bowl and stir in the toasted almonds. Refrigerate the icing for about 20 minutes to stiffen slightly.
11. Peel the waxed paper off the cake layers. Spread the top of one layer with icing, place the second layer on top and ice the top and sides of the cake. Carefully slip the cake onto a cake server or cake plate and refrigerate until a few minutes before serving time.

Note: Choose the best formed layer for the top of the cake. The texture of the icing can be adjusted for perfect spreading consistency by chilling to stiffen or leaving out at room temperature to soften. If the kitchen is very warm, prepare a bowl of ice cubes in which to set the bowl of icing while spreading it on the cake.

HAZELNUT-CHERRY TORTE

Marion Lear Swaybill

One 10" cake

Hazelnut Cake:
DRY BREAD CRUMBS
5 EGG YOLKS
1½ CUPS SUGAR
3 CUPS FINELY GROUND HAZEL-
　NUTS
4 TABLESPOONS STRONG COFFEE
6 EGG WHITES

Cherry Glaze:
1 CAN (16 OUNCES) PITTED, TART,
　RED CHERRIES

2 TABLESPOONS CORNSTARCH
⅓ CUP SUGAR
2 TABLESPOONS CHERRY LIQUEUR*

Frosting:
½ PINT HEAVY CREAM
CONFECTIONERS' SUGAR, TO TASTE
1 TEASPOON VANILLA EXTRACT

1. Preheat the oven to 350 F.
2. Butter a 10" springform pan and sprinkle it with bread crumbs.
3. Beat the egg yolks, then add the sugar and beat until it is dissolved and the mixture is thick and lemon colored. Add the nuts and coffee and stir until well blended.
4. Beat the egg whites until stiff, but not dry. Fold into the batter.
5. Pour the batter into the prepared pan and bake 40 minutes in the preheated oven.
6. Let the cake cool at room temperature in the pan on a rack. When completely cool, remove the sides of the springform and refrigerate the cake.
7. Meanwhile, make the cherry glaze. Drain the cherries and reserve the juice.
8. In a small saucepan, blend the cornstarch with ½ cup of the reserved cherry juice. Place over low heat, stirring constantly, and bring to a boil. Add the sugar and continue to cook and stir until the mixture is clear. Remove from the heat, and add the cherry liqueur.
9. Cool to room temperature, then, carefully, stir in the cherries, being careful not to bruise them.
10. Spread the cooled cherry glaze on top of the cake, leaving a 1½" border around the circumference.
11. Whip the heavy cream with the confectioners' sugar and vanilla. Evenly spread a thin layer on the sides of the cake. Fit a pastry bag with a #5 star tube and make a border around the cherries.
12. Refrigerate until ready to serve.

Note: If you are not handy with a pastry tube, spread the whipped cream softly and evenly around the cherries. Both the cake and cherry glaze can be made as much as two days in advance of assembly.

* A scant tablespoon of lemon juice may be substituted for the liqueur.

ANGEL FOOD WITH CREAM FILLING

Ruth Ellen Church

16 servings

This cake is a combination of two delectable desserts, angel food cake and old-fashioned cream pie filling. It is one of the best ways to make a party dessert of angel food.

Cake:
1½ CUPS (12 TO 14) EGG WHITES
½ TEASPOON SALT
2 TEASPOONS CREAM OF TARTAR
2 TABLESPOONS WATER
1 TEASPOON VANILLA EXTRACT
1 TEASPOON ALMOND EXTRACT
2 CUPS MINUS 2 TABLESPOONS SUGAR
1½ CUPS SIFTED CAKE FLOUR

Filling:
⅓ CUP CORNSTARCH
⅔ CUP SUGAR
¼ TEASPOON SALT
3 CUPS MILK, SCALDED
3 EGG YOLKS, LIGHTLY BEATEN
2 TABLESPOONS BUTTER
1½ TEASPOONS VANILLA EXTRACT
1 CUP HEAVY CREAM, WHIPPED

1. Preheat the oven to 375 F.
2. In a large bowl, beat the egg whites with the salt until frothy. Sprinkle on the cream of tartar and continue beating until the whites stand in soft peaks.
3. Gradually beat in the water and extracts. Fold in half of the sugar, sifting it over the surface of the egg whites 2 tablespoons at a time. Then beat until the mixture is glossy.
4. Sift together the remaining sugar and the flour two or three times.
5. Using a whisk, carefully fold the sugar-flour mixture into the egg whites, sprinkling about ¼ cup of it at a time over the meringue.
6. When the batter is well blended, pour it into an ungreased 10" angel food tube pan and bake in the preheated oven for 40 minutes. Remove the cake from the oven, invert the pan and let the cake hang until cool. Loosen it carefully with a slim, sharp knife and remove from the pan.
7. Slice the cake horizontally into four even layers and set aside. Wash the cake pan.
8. In the top of a double boiler, blend together the cornstarch, sugar and salt. Gradually add the milk, stirring constantly.
9. Cook the mixture over boiling water, stirring constantly, until thick, about 10 minutes.
10. Add a small amount of the hot mixture to the egg yolks, stir well, then turn the egg yolks into the hot mixture, stirring constantly. Cook 5 minutes, stirring occasionally.
11. Remove from the heat and add the butter and vanilla. Stir until the butter melts. Let cool and then chill.
12. Put the layers of cake back together in the clean angel food cake pan, spreading the cream filling between them and chill well.
13. Remove the pan sides and tube carefully, and transfer the filled cake to a serving plate.

Continued from preceding page

14. Spread the whipped cream around the sides and over the top of the dessert and serve.

Note: This dessert may be prepared a day ahead of time. Leave it in the mold until ready to use, then unmold and spread with the whipped cream just before serving when it is very well chilled. To cut, use a slim, sharp knife that won't squash the layers.

PEACH-PECAN SHORTCAKE-TORTE

Florence Fabricant

One 9" layer cake

6 EGGS, SEPARATED AND AT ROOM TEMPERATURE
½ TEASPOON SALT
1 TEASPOON VANILLA EXTRACT
¾ CUP SUGAR
1 CUP SIFTED ALL-PURPOSE FLOUR
1 CUP FINELY CHOPPED PECANS OR WALNUTS
1½ TABLESPOONS RUM
½ CUP STRAINED PEACH PRESERVES
2 TABLESPOONS GRAND MARNIER
1½ CUPS HEAVY CREAM
¼ CUP CONFECTIONERS' SUGAR
4 CUPS PEELED, SLICED FRESH PEACHES COVERED WITH WATER TO WHICH 3 TABLESPOONS LEMON JUICE HAS BEEN ADDED

1. Preheat the oven to 300 F.
2. Butter and flour four 9" layer cake pans.
3. Beat the egg yolks with the salt and vanilla until very light. Gradually add ½ cup of the sugar and continue beating until thick and very light, about 5 minutes. Stir in the flour and nuts, then stir in the rum.
4. Beat the egg whites until they will form soft peaks. Gradually beat in the remaining ¼ cup of sugar and continue beating until the egg whites are stiff and glossy.
5. Stir a quarter of the egg whites into the nut batter to lighten it, then gently fold in the rest.
6. Divide the batter evenly among the four baking pans, smooth the top surface of each and bake until lightly browned and springy to the touch, about 25 minutes. Cool on racks, then unmold.

   Note: If your oven cannot accommodate all four pans at one time on the same rack, bake them two at a time, keeping the unbaked batter covered until ready to use.

7. In a small saucepan, heat the preserves until completely dissolved. Stir in the Grand Marnier and simmer for 5 minutes. Brush all but about 2 tablespoons of the warm glaze on the cooled cake layers.
8. Whip the cream until softly peaked. Add the confectioners' sugar and beat until stiff.

9. Drain and dry the peach slices and arrange them on top of each cake layer.
10. Spread three of the layers with whipped cream. Assemble the three cream-filled layers of the torte, piling them one on top of another and placing the layer without the cream on top. Brush the peaches on top of the cake with the remaining glaze (warming it to dissolve, if necessary). Refrigerate the torte until ready to serve.
11. To serve, cut into thin slices with a serrated knife.

LINZERTORTE

Bianca Brown

1 torte

2¼ CUPS ALL-PURPOSE FLOUR
½ TEASPOON CINNAMON
¼ TEASPOON DOUBLE-ACTING BAKING POWDER
1 CUP CONFECTIONERS' SUGAR, APPROXIMATELY
1 CUP GRATED, BLANCHED ALMONDS
1 TEASPOON GRATED LEMON RIND
½ POUND (2 STICKS) UNSALTED BUTTER, CHILLED AND CUT INTO BITS
2 EGG YOLKS, LIGHTLY BEATEN
1 CUP THICK RASPBERRY PRESERVES
1 EGG, LIGHTLY BEATEN WITH 1 TEASPOON WATER

1. Into a bowl, sift together the flour, cinnamon and baking powder. Add 1 cup of the sugar, the almonds and lemon rind and toss to combine. Blend in the cold butter bits until the mixture resembles meal. Add the egg yolks and blend together to form a dough. Shape the dough into a ball, dust lightly with flour, wrap in waxed paper and chill for at least 2 hours.
2. With your fingers, press two-thirds of the dough into a 9''-round x 1½''-deep false-bottomed cake pan so that it covers the bottom of the pan and extends ½'' up the sides.
3. Spread the raspberry preserves evenly over the dough.
4. Cut the remaining dough into eight pieces. With your hands, roll each piece back and forth on a work surface into a long, thin cylinder and arrange them, lattice-fashion, over the preserves, pressing against the rim to secure them. Chill the torte for 45 minutes.
5. Preheat the oven to 350 F.
6. Brush the lattice and rim of the torte with the egg wash. Bake for 40 to 45 minutes, or until lightly browned. Set the pan on top of a large wide-mouthed jar and carefully slip down the outside rim. Move the torte to a rack and allow to cool for 45 minutes.
7. With a broad spatula, loosen the torte from the bottom of the cake pan and return it to the rack to cool completely.
8. Wrap the torte in foil and let it stand for 24 hours.
9. Before serving, fill the squares formed by the lattice with more preserves, if desired, and dust with confectioners' sugar.

BLACK AND WHITE TUNNEL CAKE

Paula J. Buchholz

One 10" tube cake

½ POUND (2 STICKS) BUTTER OR MARGARINE
2 CUPS SUGAR
3 EGGS
3 CUPS ALL-PURPOSE FLOUR
2 TEASPOONS BAKING POWDER
½ TEASPOON SALT
1 CUP MILK
1½ TEASPOONS VANILLA EXTRACT
¾ CUP CHOCOLATE SYRUP
¼ TEASPOON BAKING SODA

1. Preheat the oven to 350 F.
2. Butter and flour a 10" tube pan.
3. Cream the butter and sugar together until light and fluffy.
4. Add the eggs, one at a time, beating well.
5. Combine the flour, baking powder and salt and add to the creamed mixture, alternating with the milk and vanilla.
6. Pour two-thirds of the batter into the prepared tube pan.
7. Mix the chocolate syrup and baking soda with the remaining one-third batter and spoon the chocolate batter over the vanilla batter in the pan.
8. Bake until a cake tester inserted in the center comes out clean, about 55 minutes. Surprisingly, when you slice into the cake you'll find the chocolate cake completely surrounded by the vanilla. Hence, the name. This cake is rich, so slice thinly.

MARBLED 1, 2, 3, 4 CAKE

Isabel S. Cornell

One 10" tube cake

My mother-in-law, a born cook, could make soup out of stones. This is her old-fashioned pound cake with chocolate added. Like most pound cakes, this one needs no frosting and is a good companion to a cup of coffee.

½ POUND (2 STICKS) BUTTER, APPROXIMATELY
1 TEASPOON ALMOND EXTRACT
2 CUPS SUGAR
4 EGGS
3 CUPS SIFTED FLOUR
1½ TEASPOONS DOUBLE-ACTING BAKING POWDER
½ TEASPOON SALT
1 CUP PLUS 2 TABLESPOONS MILK
2 SQUARES UNSWEETENED CHOCOLATE, MELTED
1 TEASPOON VANILLA EXTRACT

1. Preheat the oven to 325 F.

2. Thoroughly butter a 10" x 4½"-deep tube pan.
3. Cream together the ½ pound of butter and almond extract, then gradually add the sugar, continuing to beat. Add the eggs, one at a time, beating very well after each addition, until the mixture is light-colored and fluffy.
4. Sift together the flour, baking powder and salt. Add to the batter in thirds, alternating with 1 cup of milk, and beating just enough to blend after each addition.
5. Combine 2 cups of the batter with the melted chocolate and vanilla; carefully stir in the remaining 2 tablespoons of milk.
6. Arrange alternating spoonfuls of dark and light batter in the pan, then draw a knife through the batter to create a marbled effect.
7. Bake in the preheated oven for about 60 to 70 minutes, until the cake tests done. Let the cake cool 10 minutes in the pan before unmolding it onto a rack to cool.

MINA THOMPSON'S BANANA LAYER CAKE

Maria Luisa Scott and Jack Denton Scott

One 9" layer cake

Cake:
2 CUPS SIFTED CAKE FLOUR
1 TEASPOON BAKING POWDER
1 TEASPOON BAKING SODA
¼ TEASPOON SALT
8 TABLESPOONS (1 STICK) BUTTER OR MARGARINE
1½ CUPS SUGAR
1 EGG YOLK PLUS 1 WHOLE EGG, WELL BEATEN
1 CUP (ABOUT 2 MEDIUM-SIZED) MASHED BANANAS

¾ CUP SOUR MILK
1 TEASPOON VANILLA EXTRACT

Butter Cream Icing:
⅓ CUP BUTTER OR MARGARINE
3½ CUPS SIFTED CONFECTIONERS' SUGAR
¼ CUP MILK
1 TEASPOON VANILLA EXTRACT
¾ CUP COARSELY CHOPPED WALNUTS

1. Preheat the oven to 375 F.
2. Butter two 9" layer cake pans. Dust them lightly with flour; invert to remove excess flour.
3. Sift together, three times, the flour, baking powder, soda and salt.
4. In a bowl, cream the butter, then add the sugar and beat until light and fluffy.
5. Add the eggs and beat well.
6. Add the bananas and beat again.
7. Add the flour mixture alternately with the milk, beating after each addition until smooth. Stir in the vanilla. Pour the batter into the pans, dividing it equally among them.
8. Bake in the preheated oven for 25 minutes, or until the cake springs back when

Continued from preceding page

    touched lightly in the center.

9. While the cake is baking, make the frosting. In a bowl, cream the butter. Mix in the sugar, adding small amounts at a time.
10. Mix in the milk and vanilla and beat until smooth. Set aside.
11. When the cake is done, place the layers on a wire rack and allow to cool in the pans for 10 minutes; then unmold onto the rack to continue cooling.
12. Frost the bottom layer with the butter cream icing. Place the second layer on top of the first and frost the top and sides with the remaining icing. Press the chopped nuts into the icing around the sides of the cake.

DELUXE CHOCOLATE LAYER CAKE

Lucy Wing

One 9" triple layer cake

3 CUPS SIFTED CAKE FLOUR
⅔ CUP UNSWEETENED COCOA
½ TEASPOON BAKING POWDER
2 TEASPOONS BAKING SODA
½ TEASPOON SALT
2 CUPS SUGAR
1 CUP VEGETABLE SHORTENING
4 LARGE EGGS
2 CUPS WATER
2 TEASPOONS VANILLA EXTRACT

Mocha Frosting:
12 TABLESPOONS (1½ STICKS) BUTTER, SOFTENED

2 TABLESPOONS UNSWEETENED COCOA
6 TO 7 CUPS (ABOUT 1¾ POUNDS) CONFECTIONERS' SUGAR*
½ CUP COLD STRONG COFFEE
1 TEASPOON VANILLA EXTRACT

PECAN HALVES (OPTIONAL)

1. Preheat the oven to 350 F.
2. Grease three 9" x 1½" layer cake pans. Line the bottom of each with a round of waxed paper. Grease the paper.
3. Sift the flour, cocoa, baking powder, baking soda and salt onto a sheet of waxed paper.
4. In the large bowl of an electric mixer, beat together the sugar, shortening and eggs at medium speed until the mixture is light and fluffy, about 3 minutes.
5. With the mixer running at low speed, add the dry ingredients alternately with the water, beginning and ending with the flour, and scraping the bowl frequently. Stir in the vanilla.
6. Pour the batter into the prepared pans.
7. Bake in the preheated oven for 30 to 35 minutes, or until the center of the cake springs back when lightly pressed.

8. Cool the layers in the pans on wire racks for 10 minutes. Loosen the cakes around the edges with a knife, and then turn the layers out onto wire racks to cool completely.
9. Meanwhile, prepare the frosting. In the large bowl of an electric mixer, beat the butter at medium speed until fluffy. Beat in the cocoa on low speed.
10. Add 6 cups of the sugar, 1 cup at a time, alternately with the coffee, beating until smooth and of a spreadable consistency. If needed, add more sugar gradually. Stir in the vanilla and mix well.
11. Fill and frost the cake and garnish with pecan halves, if desired.

* If the confectioners' sugar is lumpy, sift it.

CHOCOLATE WALNUT TORTE

Nicola Zanghi

One 9" cake

A not-too-sweet cake, perfect for late afternoon tea or coffee, from the Liguria region of Italy.

VEGETABLE OIL
¼ CUP FINE DRY BREAD CRUMBS
6 EGGS, SEPARATED
⅔ CUP SIFTED SUGAR
1⅔ CUPS SHELLED WALNUTS, FINELY GROUND
2 TABLESPOONS GRATED UNSWEETENED CHOCOLATE
¼ CUP GRATED SWEETENED CHOCOLATE
1 TABLESPOON UNSWEETENED COCOA
¼ TEASPOON VANILLA EXTRACT
GRATED RIND OF ½ LEMON

1. Preheat the oven to 375 F.
2. Brush a 9" springform pan with the vegetable oil and dust it with the bread crumbs, shaking out any excess crumbs.
3. Beat the egg yolks with the sugar until pale and fluffy.
4. Mix all of the remaining ingredients, excluding the egg whites, into the beaten egg yolks.
5. Beat the egg whites until stiff, then very gently fold them into the batter, one-quarter at a time.

    Note: The egg whites should be beaten in a copper or stainless-steel bowl; never attempt to beat eggs in an aluminum bowl.

6. Pour the batter into the prepared pan and bake for 40 minutes. Remove from the oven, allow to cool in the pan for 5 minutes, then invert onto a wire rack or serving platter.
7. Serve as is or with a lightly sweetened whipped cream. Accompany with tea, coffee or *cappuccino*.

Note: This cake serves admirably as a base chocolate cake. It also freezes well.

THREE-LAYER CAKE FOR TWO

Jane Moulton

One 5" layer cake

This triple-layer cake is just enough to last two people two meals. It's a boon to dieters who shouldn't be tempted more than twice, and to small households of one or two who can't eat an entire regulation-size cake before it goes stale. To make this mini-cake, you will need three 4½" or 5" quiche pans with removable bottoms.

Cake:
1 MEDIUM-SIZED EGG
¼ CUP SUGAR
¼ TEASPOON VANILLA EXTRACT
¼ CUP ALL-PURPOSE FLOUR
½ TEASPOON BAKING POWDER
⅛ TEASPOON SALT
1½ TEASPOONS BUTTER OR MARGARINE
2 TABLESPOONS MILK

Cherry-Cream Cheese Frosting:
1½ OUNCES CREAM CHEESE
1 TABLESPOON MARASCHINO CHERRY JUICE
1 TABLESPOON CHOPPED, DRAINED MARASCHINO CHERRIES
2½ CUPS SIFTED CONFECTIONERS' SUGAR, APPROXIMATELY
1 TABLESPOON CHOPPED PECANS OR WALNUTS

1. Preheat the oven to 350 F.
2. Grease three 4½" or 5" quiche pans with removable bottoms.
3. In a small mixer bowl, beat the egg until thick and lemon colored, about 3 minutes at high speed. Gradually add the sugar and vanilla and beat well, about 3 or 4 minutes.
4. Sift together the flour, baking powder and salt. Stir into the egg mixture until just blended.
5. In a very small saucepan, heat the butter and milk over low heat until the butter melts. Stir gently into the batter until just blended.
6. Pour the batter into the three quiche pans. Bake in the preheated oven for about 15 minutes, or until the cakes test done.
7. Meanwhile, make the frosting. In a small mixer bowl, cream the cheese and beat in the cherry juice and cherries.
8. Gradually beat in the confectioners' sugar, until the frosting is of spreading consistency.
9. When the cakes are done, cool them for 5 minutes in the pans, on a rack. Remove from the pans and cool completely on the rack.
10. Spread some frosting on the tops of the bottom and middle layers. Stack all three layers and spread the rest of the frosting around the sides and over the top. Sprinkle with chopped nuts.

Loaf, Sheet, Rolled and Specialty Cakes

EGGNOG ROULADE

Florence Fabricant

One 15" cake roll

A perfect dessert for a Christmas or New Year dinner or buffet, to go with the traditional fruit cake, *bûche de Noël* and cookies.

Cake:
6 EGGS
1 CUP SUGAR
1 CUP SIFTED CAKE FLOUR
8 TABLESPOONS (1 STICK) UNSALTED BUTTER, MELTED AND COOLED
1 TEASPOON VANILLA EXTRACT
CONFECTIONERS' SUGAR

Filling:
½ CUP GOLDEN RAISINS
½ CUP DARK RUM
2 EGG YOLKS
½ CUP SUGAR
1 TEASPOON UNFLAVORED GELATIN
¾ CUP HEAVY CREAM
½ TEASPOON GROUND NUTMEG

1. Preheat the oven to 350 F.
2. Grease a 10½" x 15½" jelly roll pan and line it with parchment or waxed paper. Grease the paper.
3. Fit the bowl of an electric mixer over, but not in, a pan of barely simmering water. Place the eggs and sugar in the bowl and stir to combine. Warm the mixture for 15 minutes, stirring occasionally. Make sure the bowl is not sitting *in* the water.
4. Fit the bowl onto the mixer and beat the warmed egg-sugar mixture at high speed for about 15 minutes, until the mixture resembles whipped cream.

    Note: If you have a mixer equipped with a water jacket, fill it with hot, not boiling, water, set the bowl containing the eggs and sugar in it and beat without heating them first.

5. Reduce the speed to low. Sift in the flour, then pour in the melted butter through a fine strainer. Add the vanilla.
6. Pour the batter into the prepared pan and spread it evenly with a spatula. Bake for 25 minutes in the preheated oven, until golden brown and the surface springs back when touched lightly.
7. On a work surface, place a sheet of waxed paper large enough to hold the cake and dust it liberally with sifted confectioners' sugar. Turn the cake out onto the waxed paper and peel off the waxed or parchment paper liner.

Continued from preceding page

8. Starting from one of the long sides of the rectangle, immediately roll the cake loosely, using the waxed paper as a guide. Set aside to cool.
9. To make the filling, soak the raisins in half of the rum.
10. Beat the egg yolks with the sugar until thick and light.
11. In a metal measuring cup, soften the gelatin in the remaining rum. Place the cup in a pan of simmering water to dissolve the gelatin.
12. Slowly add the dissolved gelatin mixture to the egg-sugar mixture, beating constantly.
13. Whip the cream and fold it into the egg-sugar mixture. Stir in the nutmeg. Refrigerate the filling for 1 hour before filling the cake.
14. When the cake has cooled and the filling is chilled, gently unroll the cake. Sprinkle it with the raisins and the rum in which they were soaking. Spread with the filling and reroll.
15. Dust with confectioners' sugar and serve at once.

FRESH GINGER CAKE

Emanuel and Madeline Greenberg

One 9" square cake

Aficionados of Oriental cooking know fresh ginger as an indispensable seasoning for savory dishes. It also adds unique flavor to this cake.

1½ CUPS SIFTED ALL-PURPOSE FLOUR
1 TEASPOON BAKING SODA
¼ TEASPOON SALT
7 TABLESPOONS SALAD OIL
½ CUP PLUS 1 TABLESPOON APPLE JUICE
½ CUP PACKED BROWN SUGAR
¼ CUP LIGHT MOLASSES
¼ CUP DARK CORN SYRUP
1 EGG
3 TABLESPOONS GRATED FRESH GINGER*
WHIPPED CREAM (OPTIONAL)
CANDIED GINGER, FINELY CHOPPED (OPTIONAL)

1. Preheat the oven to 350 F.
2. Grease and flour a 9"-square baking pan.
3. Sift together the flour, baking soda and salt. Set aside.
4. In a mixing bowl, combine the salad oil and apple juice. Beat in the sugar, molasses and corn syrup. Beat in the egg. Add the ginger and dry ingredients and mix well.
5. Pour the batter into the prepared pan. Bake for 30 to 35 minutes, or until the cake is firm to the touch in the center and has pulled away slightly from the sides of the pan. Cool in the pan for about 5 minutes, then turn out onto a cake rack.

6. Cut into squares to serve, while the cake is still warm or at room temperature. For special occasions, serve topped with whipped cream and a sprinkle of finely chopped candied ginger.

* Don't try to substitute ground ginger—it's not the same. Fresh ginger is available in Oriental and Hispanic markets and in many gourmet food shops.

BABA AU RHUM

Carol Cutler

12 babas

These sweet, leavened cakes have some of the characteristics of *brioche*. The *baba* is said to have been made famous by King Stanislaus of Poland, who was so fond of them that he had them prepared for his State Visit to France in the early 17th century.

Babas:
1½ CUPS WHITE FLOUR
1 PACKAGE ACTIVE DRY YEAST
2 TABLESPOONS TEPID WATER
1 TEASPOON SALT
2 TABLESPOONS SUGAR
2 LARGE EGGS
4 TABLESPOONS (½ STICK) BUTTER, MELTED AND COOLED

Rum Syrup:
2 CUPS WATER
1 CUP SUGAR
½ CUP DARK RUM

Apricot Glaze:
3 TABLESPOONS APRICOT JAM
2 TEASPOONS WATER, APPROXIMATELY

1. Put the flour in a deep mixing bowl, make a well in the center and put the yeast in the well. Add the tepid water and let it stand a few seconds to dissolve the yeast.
2. Add the salt, sugar and eggs to the well. Using the tips of the fingers, blend together the ingredients in the center, then gradually incorporate the flour. When all of the ingredients have been worked together, knead for at least 5 minutes.
3. Add the cooled, melted butter, and knead again to incorporate it.
4. Place the dough in a greased bowl, cover, and let stand in a warm place for 1½ to 2 hours, or until the dough has doubled in bulk. Test by pressing your finger in the center of the dough; the depression should remain.
5. Preheat the oven to 375 F.
6. Butter 12 *baba* molds, custard cups, or a 12-cup muffin tin.
7. Deflate the dough by kneading gently with your fingertips. Break off enough dough to fill each mold one-third full, and press the dough lightly into the bottom of the mold.
8. Place the uncovered molds in a warm place and let the dough rise again until it expands ¼" above the tops of the molds.

Continued from preceding page

9. Bake at once for about 15 minutes, or until the *babas* are nicely browned and have shrunk slightly from the sides of the molds.
10. While the *babas* are baking, make the rum syrup. Boil 2 cups of water and the sugar together for 2 minutes; remove from the heat and pour in the rum.
11. Before the *babas* have cooled completely, prick the tops and sides of the warm cakes and place them in a deep dish. Pour the lukewarm rum syrup over them and let stand, basting occasionally. (A bulb baster works well for this.) Drain on a rack.
12. While the *babas* are soaking, make the apricot glaze. Force the apricot jam through a strainer into a small pan, add approximately 2 teaspoons of water and place over medium heat. Mix with a wire whisk until the jam has melted.
13. Brush this glaze over the tops of the drained *babas*.
14. *Babas* are best eaten the day they are prepared, but will keep in the refrigerator for a day or two.

OLD-FASHIONED CARROT CAKE

Ruth Spear

12 to 15 servings

Like many spice cakes, carrot cake is even better the day after it is baked, when the flavors have had a chance to ripen. Wrap well in plastic wrap after cooling, and store unrefrigerated for a day, if possible. The cake keeps well for a week (if you can keep it around that long!).

6 TO 8 CARROTS, SCRAPED
2 CUPS SUGAR
1½ CUPS CORN OIL
4 EGGS, LIGHTLY BEATEN
2 CUPS ALL-PURPOSE FLOUR
1 TEASPOON SALT
2 TEASPOONS BAKING SODA
2 TEASPOONS CINNAMON
½ TEASPOON NUTMEG
½ TEASPOON ALLSPICE
½ CUP CHOPPED WALNUTS

Butter Cream Sauce:
8 TABLESPOONS (1 STICK) UNSALTED BUTTER, SOFTENED
1 PACKAGE (8 OUNCES) CREAM CHEESE
2 CUPS CONFECTIONERS' SUGAR
2 TEASPOONS VANILLA EXTRACT

1. Preheat the oven to 325 F.
2. Butter a 13" x 9" x 2" baking dish.
3. Grate enough carrots to yield 3 cups. Set aside.
4. In an electric mixer or by hand, mix together the sugar, oil and eggs. (If working by hand, beat the eggs well first.)
5. Sift together the flour, salt, soda and spices. Add the flour mixture to the egg mixture in four equal parts, blending well after each addition.

6. Fold in the carrots and nuts and pour the batter into the prepared pan.
7. Bake in the preheated oven for 60 to 70 minutes.
8. While the cake is baking, cream the butter until light and fluffy.
9. Mash the cream cheese with a fork and work it into the butter. Add the confectioners' sugar and vanilla and beat vigorously, until blended.

    Note: To make in a food processor, cut the butter into chunks and whirl for 4 or 5 seconds. Add the cream cheese and whirl again briefly. Add the sugar and vanilla and blend a few seconds more.

10. When the cake is done, cool on a rack. Serve the cake, cut into squares, with the butter cream sauce.

Note: The cake may be made in a buttered bundt pan in which case it should bake at 350 F. for 55 to 60 minutes.

CHOCOLATE CHIFFON CAKE

Marion Lear Swaybill

One 10" cake

24 LADYFINGERS
2 PACKAGES (2 TABLESPOONS) UNFLAVORED GELATIN
1 CUP SUGAR
½ TEASPOON SALT
2 CUPS MILK
6 EGGS, SEPARATED

12 OUNCES SEMISWEET CHOCOLATE, BROKEN INTO SMALL PIECES
2 TEASPOONS VANILLA EXTRACT
2 CUPS HEAVY CREAM
CONFECTIONERS' SUGAR
GRATED CHOCOLATE

1. Lightly butter a 10" springform pan.
2. Separate the ladyfingers into halves and line the sides and bottom of the pan with them. (The rounded side of the ladyfingers should be against the pan.)
3. In the top of a double boiler, combine the gelatin, half of the sugar and the salt. Stir in the milk, egg yolks and chocolate. Place over boiling water and cook, stirring constantly, until the gelatin dissolves and the chocolate melts, about 6 minutes.
4. Remove from the heat and whisk until the chocolate is thoroughly incorporated. Stir in the vanilla, then chill in the refrigerator until the mixture mounds slightly when dropped from a spoon.
5. Beat the egg whites until stiff but not dry. Gradually add the remaining ½ cup of sugar and beat until stiff. Fold into the chocolate-gelatin mixture.
6. Whip 1 cup of cream and fold it into the chocolate mixture. Pour into the pan lined with ladyfingers, cover and refrigerate overnight.
7. Shortly before serving, whip the remaining cup of cream and sweeten it slightly with a bit of confectioners' sugar. Unmold the cake and spread the whipped cream over the top. Decorate with grated chocolate.

ARKANSAS SPECIAL DESSERT

Isabel S. Cornell

One 9" pie-shaped cake

Several versions of this recipe swept the country about 30 years ago. One was called Harry Truman's favorite dessert. It is a light yet filling dessert that is popular with everyone. This version is easy to assemble, and shredding the apples is not only faster than chopping but they won't darken as quickly.

½ CUP FLOUR
1 TEASPOON DOUBLE-ACTING BAKING POWDER
¼ TEASPOON SALT
2 EGGS
1 CUP SUGAR
GRATED RIND OF 1 LEMON
1 TEASPOON VANILLA EXTRACT
1 TO 1¼ CUPS PEELED AND SHREDDED CRISP APPLES
⅓ CUP FINELY CHOPPED NUTS
WHIPPED CREAM OR ICE CREAM (OPTIONAL)

1. Preheat the oven to 325 F.
2. Butter a 9" glass pie dish.
3. Sift together the flour, baking powder and salt. Set aside.
4. Beat the eggs, then add the sugar, lemon rind and vanilla and continue beating until the mixture is light colored and fluffy.
5. Add and quickly beat in the flour mixture.
6. Fold in the apples and nuts.
7. Turn into the buttered pie dish and bake in the preheated oven for 35 to 40 minutes, until puffed and lightly browned.
8. Serve warm, cooled or cold, with whipped cream or vanilla ice cream, if desired.

COFFEE ALMOND SPONGE CAKE

Nan Mabon

One 8" cake

12 TABLESPOONS (1½ STICKS) UNSALTED BUTTER, APPROXIMATELY
6 OUNCES (ABOUT ¾ CUP) PLUS 1 TABLESPOON SUGAR
3 EGGS
1 CUP SIFTED FLOUR
PINCH OF SALT
4 TABLESPOONS DARK RUM OR BRANDY
1 CUP STRONG COFFEE
1 CUP HEAVY CREAM
½ TEASPOON VANILLA EXTRACT
½ CUP SLICED ALMONDS, TOASTED

1. Preheat the oven to 375 F.
2. Butter the inside of an 8"-round cake pan and cut a circle of parchment or waxed paper to fit the bottom. Also butter the paper and then dust the pan with a light coating of flour, shaking out the excess.

3. Cream the 12 tablespoons butter and ¾ cup of the sugar together until light and fluffy.

4. Add the eggs, one at a time, to the butter-sugar mixture (don't be alarmed if it looks somewhat curdled). With a large metal spoon, gently fold in the sifted flour and the salt.

5. Turn this mixture into the prepared pan and bake in the center of the oven for 25 minutes. When the cake is done, a cake tester inserted in the middle should come out clean. Cool the cake in the tin for about 10 minutes. Turn it out onto a plate, remove the paper, then put it back into the tin, bottom-side up. (The porous bottom will easily absorb the syrup called for in the next step.)

6. Mix the rum (or brandy) with the coffee and pour it over the cake. Let it sit for a few minutes, until well absorbed.

7. Carefully turn the cake out onto a serving platter and wipe off any excess coffee that dribbles onto it. Slide strips of waxed paper under the edges of the cake to keep the platter clean.

8. Whip the cream until very stiff with the remaining tablespoon of sugar and the vanilla.

9. Put about 4 tablespoons of the whipped cream in a pastry decorator fitted with a star tip and smooth the rest over the top and sides of the cake. Place the almonds in porcupine-like rows around the sides of the cake. Make a band of cream with the pastry decorator around the top edge of the cake, then lay another band of almonds inside the ring of cream.

10. Serve immediately. This cake is best eaten right away, but it can be stored in the refrigerator, well covered, for a day or so.

GINGER BREAD

Maurice Moore-Betty

About 8 servings

Ginger bread of this kind has been made in the North of England for two hundred years or more. It should be heavy and soggy.

10 OUNCES (ABOUT 2½ CUPS) ALL-PURPOSE FLOUR
1 TEASPOON GROUND GINGER
½ TEASPOON GROUND CINNAMON
PINCH OF SALT
4 OUNCES (ABOUT ¾ CUP) CHOPPED DATES
2 OUNCES (ABOUT 5½ TABLESPOONS) GOLDEN RAISINS

6 TABLESPOONS (¾ STICK) BUTTER
5 FLUID OUNCES LIGHT MOLASSES
1 EGG
4 OUNCES (1 CUP UNPACKED) DARK BROWN SUGAR
¾ TABLESPOON BAKING SODA
3 TABLESPOONS MILK

1. Preheat the oven to 325 F.

2. Butter and sugar a 10'' round or square cake tin.

3. Sift together the flour, ginger, cinnamon and salt. Add the dates and raisins.

Continued from preceding page

4. In a small saucepan, melt the butter and molasses together over gentle heat and cool slightly.
5. Beat the egg and brown sugar together.
6. Add the melted butter and molasses syrup to the flour alternately with the egg-sugar mixture.
7. Dissolve the baking soda in the milk, add to the batter and beat well, until the mixture is soft. Add a little water if necessary.
8. Pour the batter into the prepared cake tin. Bake on the middle rack of the oven for 1½ to 2 hours, or until a toothpick inserted in the center comes out dry.
9. Partially cool the cake in the pan, then remove to a wire rack.

CHOCOLATE-MOKA HAZELNUT CAKE

Nan Mabon

One 9" cake

FINE, DRY BREAD CRUMBS
6 OUNCES SWEETENED CHOCOLATE
8 TABLESPOONS (1 STICK) UNSALTED BUTTER
¾ CUP SUGAR
4 LARGE EGGS, SEPARATED
¾ CUP HAZELNUTS (FILBERTS), TOASTED, SKINS REMOVED AND GROUND

¼ CUP UNSWEETENED COCOA
1 TEASPOON INSTANT COFFEE
1 CUP WHIPPING CREAM
½ TEASPOON VANILLA EXTRACT

1. Preheat the oven to 375 F.
2. Lightly butter a 9"-round cake pan. Cut a 9" circle out of parchment or waxed paper and put it on the bottom of the buttered pan. Butter the paper also, then sprinkle the pan with dried bread crumbs, shaking out any excess.
3. Melt the chocolate in the top of a double boiler. Remove from the heat and let cool.
4. Cream the butter with ½ cup of the sugar until light and fluffy. Add the egg yolks, one at a time, stirring well after each addition. Blend in the melted chocolate, then the hazelnuts.
5. Whip the egg whites until they hold stiff peaks and gently fold them into the batter.
6. Pour into the prepared pan and bake for 45 minutes. Let the cake cool in the pan 10 minutes, then turn it out onto a rack, remove the paper and cool another 15 minutes.
7. Stir the cocoa, the remaining ¼ cup sugar and the coffee into the cream along with the vanilla, and chill in the refrigerator for 30 minutes.

8. Place the cooled cake on a serving platter and slip pieces of waxed paper under the edges to keep the platter clean while the cake is frosted.
9. Beat the chilled cream mixture until very stiff and place it in a pastry bag fitted with a star tube.
10. Cover the entire cake with rosettes of the chocolate frosting. Remove the paper under the cake.

    Note: The frosting can also be spread with a spatula if you lack a pastry bag, or the patience to make the rosettes. Save a few whole, toasted nuts to decorate the top if you opt for this method.
11. This cake will keep for a few days stored in the refrigerator, but be sure to bring it to room temperature before serving.

ALMOND BUTTER CREAM CAKE (CHARLOTTE MALAKOFF)

Alma Lach

14 servings

12 COMMERCIAL LADYFINGERS
½ POUND (2 STICKS) BUTTER
1½ CUPS SUGAR
½ TEASPOON SALT
2½ CUPS GROUND ALMONDS
1 TEASPOON VANILLA EXTRACT

½ CUP KIRSCH
2 CUPS WHIPPING CREAM
½ CUP CONFECTIONERS' SUGAR
WHIPPED CREAM (OPTIONAL)
CANDIED VIOLETS OR CHERRIES
(OPTIONAL)

1. Cut an 8''-diameter circle of waxed paper and fit it into the bottom of an 8'' springform pan.
2. Trim one rounded end of the ladyfingers straight across to make them stand upright. Separate the ladyfingers into halves (commercial ladyfingers have already been split) and stand them up, trimmed ends down and rounded sides out, around the sides of the springform.
3. In a large mixing bowl, cream the butter, sugar, salt and almonds together and beat until light and fluffy. Add the vanilla and kirsch and continue to beat.
4. Whip the cream until stiff, and then beat in the confectioners' sugar. Fold into the butter-almond mixture.
5. Fill the ladyfinger-lined pan with the cream mixture. Cover and refrigerate for at least 8 hours.
6. Release the cake from the springform pan and invert it onto a serving plate. Remove the waxed paper. Decorate with whipped cream and a few candied violets or candied cherry halves, if desired. Cut into wedges to serve.

CHOCOLATE SWISS ROLL

Rona Deme

One 9" cake roll

½ CUP PLUS 1 TABLESPOON CAKE FLOUR
½ CUP PLUS 1 TABLESPOON COCOA POWDER (DROSTE'S, IF POSSIBLE)
¾ TEASPOON BAKING POWDER
½ TEASPOON SALT
6 EGGS, SEPARATED
¾ CUP PLUS ⅓ CUP SUGAR
1½ TEASPOONS VANILLA EXTRACT
CONFECTIONERS' SUGAR
3 CUPS HEAVY CREAM, WHIPPED

1. Preheat the oven to 400 F.
2. Line a jelly-roll pan (approximately 14" x 9" x 1") with waxed or parchment paper. Set aside.
3. Sift together, three times, the flour, cocoa powder, baking powder and salt.
4. Beat the egg whites until stiff, but not dry. Gradually fold in the sugar.
5. Beat the egg yolks until thick and lemon colored. Blend in the vanilla extract.
6. Fold the yolks very carefully into the egg whites. Then fold in the flour-cocoa mixture.
7. Pour the batter into the prepared pan and spread it evenly. Bake for 12 minutes.
8. Turn the cake out onto a linen towel dusted with confectioners' sugar and remove the waxed or parchment paper.
9. Allow the cake to cool, then spread with the whipped cream and roll carefully, starting at one end and using the towel to lift and guide the sheet of cake.
10. You may trim the ends of the cake before serving, but it looks more like a log if they are left as is. Dust the roll with confectioners' sugar and arrange on a bed of ferns.